AF324601

taj forer

For Mrs. H

taj forer

threefold sun

CHARTA

Design
Daniela Meda

Editorial Coordination
Filomena Moscatelli

Editing
Emily Ligniti
Libby May

Copywriting and Press Office
Silvia Palombi Arte&Mostre, Milano

Sales Department
Antonia De Besi

US Office
Francesca Sorace

Cover
Young farmer, Fair Oaks, California

ISBN-10: 88-8158-635-5
ISBN-13: 978-8158-635-6

Printed in Italy

Edizioni Charta srl

via della Moscova, 27
20121 Milano
Tel. +39-026598098/026598200
Fax +39-026598577
e-mail: edcharta@tin.it

US Office
New York City, Tribeca
Tel. +1-313-406-8468
e-mail: international@chartaartbooks.it

www.chartaartbooks.it

Acknowledgments

This book is dedicated to Mrs. Eileen Hohmouth-Lemonick. Thank you for challenging me from the very beginning.

I am grateful beyond words to all the people, schools, farms, and families that welcomed and supported me during the process of making these photographs.
Thank you to the following individuals: Joel Sternfeld for your continued commitment to my work—I see the world as a better place thanks to you. Kate Svajian, my beautiful wife and best friend, your understanding and patience continues to amaze me. My parents, Douglas and Nancy, for your unconditional love and for allowing me the space to grow. Leif, my "number one brother," for being so free and inspiring. elin o'Hara slavick for your friendship and honest insight—we all need comrades! Carol Mavor, I won't write much as my words seem completely incompetent next to yours—however, from the first time I heard you read your beautiful writing on photography, something strange and wonderful began to unfold. My dear friend Michael Itkoff, your spark and passion for photography meets my own in ways that only you can understand. Giuseppe Liverani for believing in my work and making such a beautiful book out of it. My dealers Yossi Milo at Yossi Milo Gallery and Chloë Seymore and Teka Selman at Branch Gallery—you are all a joy to work with. Allen Thomas, Jr. for starting to collect my work "just in time." Larry Wheeler for your friendship, excitement, introductions, and so many wonderful conversations—I look forward to many more. Last but not least, I must thank David Heberlein, my Waldorf school teacher, you probably know me better than I know myself.
There are countless others who helped make this book a reality and I am grateful for all you have done.

This project was partially funded by the Rudolf Steiner and Mary Duke Biddle Trent Semans Foundations.

Contents

Utopia:
Red, Round, and Spelled with an "E," Taj Forer's *Threefold Sun*

Carol Mavor

I move. From early on we are searching. All we do is crave, cry out.
Do not have what we want.
Ernst Bloch[1]

Nothing much happens in the land of *Threefold Sun*.[2] And yet there are traces of both physical and spiritual lives lived: a Zenful pile of well-used gardening tools; colorful galoshes and raincoats, shorn for indoor enlightenment, residing along an unremarkable wall painted a remarkable blue; a chalkboard message that professes the heavenly joy of an immaterial life governed by the spiritual scepter; a bit of blood in the nostrils of a beautiful boy baptized with everyday dirt.

I am moved.

If you give *Threefold Sun* the solar time it deserves, if you allow yourself the slow time to slowly *move* towards its handsome, calm work, you just might be caught off guard—if you are lucky. If you are lucky, these pictures will touch you with their mud and snow and blue juniper berries, their green cabbages and sun-baked farmer, their crusty gnome holes and missing maypole ribbons: they are pictures made of nothing at all but cool starlight and warm sunlight. (As is often remarked, the etymology of "photo-graph" is "light-writing.")

---

1. Ernst Bloch, *The Principle of Hope*, trans. Neville Plaice, Stephen Plaice, and Paul Knight. Oxford: Basil Blackwell, 1986, vol. 1, p. 21. Hereafter, citations to this edition will appear with the volume and page number in parentheses in the body of the text. There are three volumes to this edition. First published in German as *Das Prinzip Hoffnug* (Frankfurt am Main: Suhrkamp Verlag, 1969).
2. Some readers may hear in this essay a delicate echo of Chantal Akerman's handsome 1975 film *Jeanne Dielman, 23 Quai du Commerce, 1080 Bruxelles*. Ivone Margulies's *Nothing Happens: Chantal Akerman's Hyperrealist Everyday* (Durham: Duke University Press, 1996) is a full expression of the film's richness. See also my essay "The *Writerly* Artist: Beautiful, Boring and Blue," in Amelia Jones, ed., *A Companion to Contemporary Art Since 1945*. Oxford: Blackwell, 2006, pp. 271–295.

I am touched by light.

Taj Forer's entelechy-containing photographs take my hand and lead me to a spiritual place. Once there, I can accept that I do not yet know what I am looking for. I look around. I cruise the pictures. At first glance: banal. Nothing. I stare. I imagine. In my mind's eye, I sit next to the boy in *Waiting for mom after school*. But, I am *not* waiting for mom. I am waiting to wish. And I suddenly find myself to be in just the right place, the *just* place of waiting and wishing for something to find me. On the bench, in the cabbage field, in the eurythmy room without people, at the father and daughter dance without fathers and daughters, in the classroom without children, on the orange-striped couch next to the Waldorf school teachers, in the tree house, in the little blue playhouse—this is the just place, the wishing place, of *Threefold Sun*, this is the place where something can find you. In the words of the photographer Emmet Gowin: "It is not what I came for, but it is what came to me."[3]

And the place of *Threefold Sun* turns out to be much more beautiful than I thought.

I begin to play. *Serio ludere* (to play seriously).[4]

Beauty is there in the maypole, bare and alone in the snow. Beauty is there in the obscured child who stands at the bottom of a yellow ladder leaning against an ugly temporary building. Beauty is there where you can find it, like a child might. "Green and blue runs the lizard, something elusively flies as a butterfly. Even the stones are alive . . . Play is transformation" (Bloch I, 21).

Taj and his brother Leif were raised by parents who were independent-minded enough and spiritual enough to send their two boys to a Waldorf school, a non-tradition-

3. From a lecture given by Emmet Gowin at the University of North Carolina, Chapel Hill, October 20, 2003.
4. For the relationship between "serious play" and the concept of utopian practice, see George M. Logan and Robert M. Adam, "Introduction," in Thomas More, *Utopia*, eds. George M. Logan and Robert M. Adam, rev. ed. Cambridge: Cambridge University Press, 1988, pp. xi–xxix.

al academic environment in which they would be given the freedom to be what the philosopher Rudolf Steiner described as "childlike enough." Steiner, whose teachings are at the epicenter of a Waldorf education, was the founder of anthroposophy, a form of theosophy based on spiritual science (from *anthro*, human, and *sophy*, wisdom), and also an artist-architect—his famed Gaudiesque *Goetheanum* was built in Dornach, Switzerland, in the late 1920s to house the Anthroposophical Society.[5] That Steiner could never have imagined Forer's large, color prints as an outcome of his teachings was a probability that he himself embraced: "the best thing we can achieve, as teachers," he wrote, "is to be able to face perfectly calmly the thought of the child becoming as different from us as possible."[6]

Now, this "education towards freedom,"[7] beautiful and banal, is taught to us through Forer's photographs of American Waldorf schools and the biodynamic farming system that Steiner also founded. Everyday calmness is held by a palette, at once serene and vibrant, that echoes the Goethean color theory absorbed by every Waldorf child. Beauty is present where we might expect it (a wall of sunny children's paintings, a tree house), but mostly where we don't (a slightly deflated yellow ball in a cement play yard, a sledding hill with not enough snow). Utopia is peacefully waiting: as an unseen ball on the roof; as a glimmer of brightness; as a patch of color; as the touch of mud.

Utopia (*u*=not, *topos*=place)

At the very beginning Thomas More designated utopia as a place,
an island in the distant South Seas . . . but I am not there.
Ernst Bloch[8]

5. For an excellent discussion of theosophy, its history, and its relationship to anthroposophy and South Asian religiosity, see Srnivas Aravamudan's brilliant and dense *Guru English: South Asian Religion in a Cosmopolitan Language*. Princeton and Oxford: Princeton University Press, 2006, pp. 105–141.
6. Rudolf Steiner, *Art as in the Light of Mystery Wisdom, Eight Lectures Given in Dornach Between 28 December 1914 and 4 January 1915*, with an introduction by Marie Steiner, trans. P. Wehrle and J. Collis. London: Rudolf Steiner Press, 1984, p. 127.
7. See Frans Carlgren, *Education towards Freedom: Rudolf Steiner Education, A Survey of the Work of Waldorf Schools Throughout the World*, with prefaces by Rodolf Grosse and Alan Howard. East Grinstead, UK: Langthorn Press, 1976. First published in German as *Erzienhung zur Freiheit*. Stuttgart: Verlag Fried Geistesleben, 1972.
8. Ernst Bloch, "Something's Missing: A Discussion between Ernst Bloch and Theodor W. Adorno on the Contradictions of Utopian Longing (1964)," in Ernst Bloch, *The Utopian Function of Art and Literature: Selected Essays*, trans. Jack Zipes and Frank Mecklenburg. Cambridge, Massachusetts and London: MIT Press, 1988, p. 3.

Forer's utopia is realized and generated by imagination. It is an island, with its own archipelago of Waldorf schools, play yards, red balls, yellow balls, chalkboards, two farmers (one shirtless, the other shoeless), a few children, some adolescents, an empty eurythmy room, a couple of benevolent teachers, a teacher's office, a dining room, a laundry line, a parking lot with a covered car. Just as the wishful child can find that "the playroom floor becomes a forest of wild animals or a lake on which every chair is a boat" (Bloch I, 3), so, too, can the viewer of *Threefold Sun* find its oceans.

I discover not the real ocean, but the poetics of an ocean in the true blue sky of the *Young farmer*, or in the turquoise blue wall of *Boots and raincoats*. I find the sea in the chalky blue playhouse that stands afar in the dirt: a child's oasis in a school near the sea (in San Diego, California), but without a view of the sea. Likewise, I am sure that the open blue sea is in the heart of not only *Father-Daughter Dance*, but also *Dance floor, Valentine's Day*. (It is said that the blood of the heart is blue inside.)

Initiation into the utopia of *Threefold Sun* means remembering oneself as spiritual and immaterial, as blue as the heavens, the sea, and the imagination. (Blue is devout and divine. "Blue is the first color to strike the visitor as he enters the Arena Chapel . . . Such a blue takes hold of the viewer."[9] And blue, in the words of Rebecca Solnit, "is the color of longing for the distances you never arrive in, for the blue world."[10] Blue is memory and longing.)

This island is a little planet: it sets me into a daydream. It is a space of imagination for the viewer. Cluttered with nothingness, these photographs of the everyday are curiously comprised of mostly empty spaces, whose emptiness is sometimes magnified by an emphasis on empty materials: the yellow and red synthetic balls; a nylon green garden hose; a school's metal and plastic boxy classroom (a temporary cost-

9. Julia Kristeva, "Giotto's Joy," in Leon S. Roudiez, ed., *Desire in Language: A Semiotic Approach to Literature and Art*, trans. Thomas Gora, Alice Jardine, and Leon S. Roudiez. New York: Columbia University Press, 1980, p. 224. First published in French as *Polyogue*. Paris: Éditions du Seuil, 1977.
10. Rebecca Solnit, *A Field Guide to Getting Lost*. London: Penguin, 2005, p. 30.

saving expansion); the concrete playground of con-temporary life; blue plastic milk carton crates. (Roland Barthes describes plastic as "the product of chemistry, not of nature . . . at once gross and hygienic, it destroys all the pleasure, the sweetness, the humanity of touch."[11])

Forer's images are different from, but not entirely different from, Eugène Atget's (1857–1927) photographs of cleared-out Paris. Both draw on an emptiness that *suggests* that something is going to happen. Empty but generous, these photographs provide what the great utopian Marxist theorist Ernst Bloch called "anticipatory illumination" (*Vor-Schein*): a glimpse at the more perfect, utopian future offered by the work of art or litera-ture.[12] ("As a poet, Bloch is perhaps a poet of light."[13])

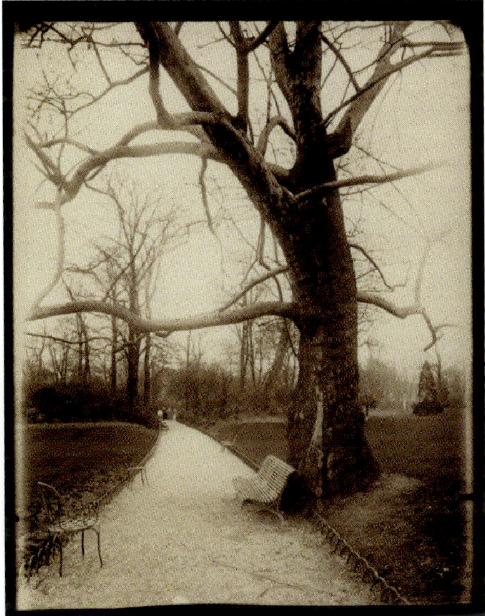

Eugène Atget (1857–1927),
Parc Monceau (8e arr) 1901–02.
Courtesy George Eastman House.

11. Roland Barthes, *Mythologies*, trans. Annette Lavers. New York: Hill & Wang, 1972, p. 54. First published in French as *Mythologies*. Paris: Éditions du Seuil, 1957.
12. And for Bloch this includes colportage: "the cheap materials sold by the colporteur or traveling bookseller of the seventeenth through nineteenth centuries. The colporteur carried bibles, chapbooks, cookbooks, primers, medical books, calendars, manuals, prayer books, romances, fairy tales, and adventure books"; see Jack Zipes, "Introduction," in Ernst Bloch, *The Utopian Function of Art and Literature: Selected Essays*, trans. Jack Zipes and Frank Mecklenburg. Cambridge, Massachusetts and London: MIT Press, 1988, p. xxxvii.
13. Neville Plaice, Stephen Plaice, and Paul Knight, "Translators' Introduction," in *The Principle of Hope*, trans. Neville Plaice, Stephen Plaice, and Paul Knight. Oxford: Basil Blackwell, 1986, vol. 1, p. xxxi.

But Forer's art goes one step further with its anticipatory illuminations of earthly concrete utopias (the Waldorf schools and the biodynamic farms). We find hope through the glimmer of light, the splendor of starkness, the attractiveness of openness, color bland and bright, the prospect of ugliness turned inside out and vice versa. (In Thomas More's *Utopia*, 1516, chamber pots are made of gold and silver. Pearls, diamonds, and garnets are mere playthings for children.[14]) Forer's images illuminate the possibilities of a different life: a life enlightened by new education and new eco-tending of the earth. I find a genuine back-to-the-future newness.

Threefold Sun thus becomes a *spiritual* space for me.

Ocean Found

By way of the blue serenity, the reward for spending the long time necessary to become, if not a full-blown initiate, at least an honorary member of *Threefold Sun*, you might be lucky enough to encounter the spiritual ocean in every oceanless photograph. Perhaps you will find it in the clouds of *Laundry*. After all, "wishes are aroused by the fairy-tale qualities of nature, especially by clouds . . . the cloud is not only castle or ice mountain to the fairy-tale gaze, but it is also an island in the sea of heaven or a ship."[15] A cloud as a ship in the sky becomes the slow sun-boat to *Threefold Sun*. I see a glimpse of it in *Sun-boat with people in it*, drawn a long time ago by a Waldorf child, now grown.

The title *Threefold Sun* comes from a lecture that Steiner gave in 1922. Steiner's "threefold sun" is the sun of the past (which was once spiritual, elemental, *and* earthly).

14. Thomas More, *Utopia*, eds. George M. Logan and Robert M. Adam, rev. ed. Cambridge: Cambridge University Press, 1988, p. 61.
15. Ernst Bloch, "Better Castles in the Sky at the Country Fair and Circus, in Fairy Tales and Colportage (1959)," in Ernst Bloch, *The Utopian Function of Art and Literature: Selected Essays, Op. cit.*, p. 175.

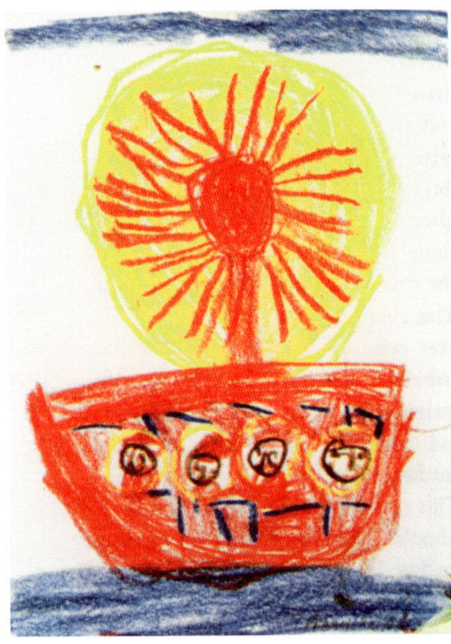

Child's drawing from Frans Carlgren,
Education towards Freedom, (Sussex,
UK: Lanthorn Press, 1981).
Courtesy Rudolf Steiner Verlag.

Steiner encourages us to look back and behold this threefold sun, now lost to our despiri-
tualized culture, so that we might possess the mysteries of human evolution and move forward to become, finally, "proper human beings, living and working and above all enjoying
themselves."[16] Bloch calls this *novum* (genuinely new).[17]

Fairy Tales

Floating slowly from one calm image to another, *Threefold Sun* often evokes for
me what Charles Clifford's photograph *Alhambra (Grenada)* (1854–1856) evoked for

16. Plaice, Plaice, and Knight, "Translator's Introduction," *Op. cit.*, p. xxxiii, on the subject of Bloch's forward thinking. Despite some
shared sentiments on hope for the future, Bloch was very critical of Steiner, a complicated topic that I take up briefly later in this
essay.
17. As Zipes writes: "Bloch used the term *Novum* in various ways to demarcate the horizon line drawn by works that open up genuinely new possibilities to move forward in the world experiment. The *Novum* as the startling and unpredictable new is always at
the forefront of human experience and indicates the qualitative reutilization of the cultural heritage"; see Zipes, "Introduction," *Op.
cit.*, p. xxxvii.

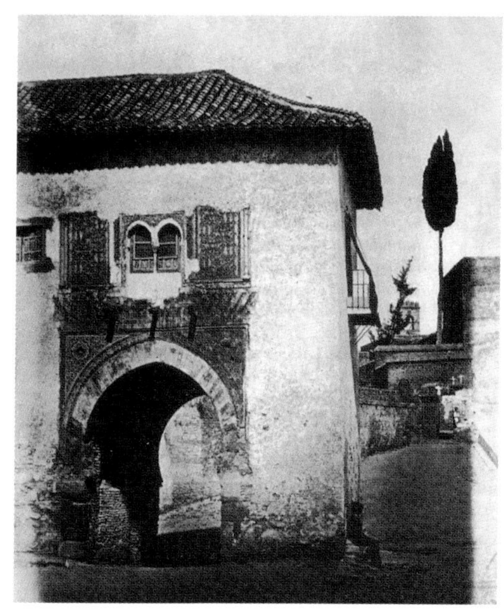

Alhambra (Grenada) (1854–1856), photograph by Charles Clifford, as reproduced in *Camera Lucida: Reflections on Photography*, translated by Richard Howard (New York: Hill and Wang, 1981). Originally published in French as *La chambre claire: Note sur la photographie* (Paris: Éditions du Seuil, 1980). Reprinted by permission of Georges Borchardt, Inc.

Barthes in *Camera Lucida*: daydreams of home. *"C'est là je voudrais vivre . . ."* (I want to live there), writes Barthes under Clifford's stunning black-and-white photograph of the famed pinkish-reddish Moorish palace/fortress (Alhambra means "the red" in Arabic.) When I look at the two girls in *Girls in straw fort*, sitting in their giant nest that they made for themselves, I think: "I want to live there." Looking at these girls in their nest—or looking at the full and tangled branches that sprout beautiful, little blue, magical fruits as they hold the peopleless tree house—or at the red tidiness of *Cleaning supplies*—or at the Little-Red-Riding-Hood quality of *Kitchen table*—or at the tiny *Gnome houses* carved out with magical rocks (with Bloch's enchanted animistic words—"even the stones are alive"—echoing in me again), I think (I think like Barthes): "I want to live there."

It is the stuff of fairy tales.

Fairy tales anchor Bloch's concept of utopia. They are the first boats we take from home, while staying at home, as we begin to imagine utopia. Fairy tales can "illuminate the possibilities for rearranging social and political relations so they engender *Heimat* (homeland), Bloch's word for the home that we have all sensed, but have never experienced or known. For Bloch, *Heimat* is utopia."[18] "Once upon a time," Bloch tells us, "means in a fairy-tale manner not only the past, but a more colorful or easier somewhere else."[19]

"One of the frequent prejudices held against Waldorf schools is that the children are told too many fairy tales."[20] In fact, fairy tales are part of the "Main Lesson" for the entire Grade One (first grade). This embracing of imaginative literature continues to be part of the child's education, in one form or another, for the entire first five years: Grade Two is devoted to fables and legends; Grade Three to selected stories from the Old Testament; Grade Four to stories from Nordic mythology; Grade Five to Greek mythology and legends from ancient India, Persia, Babylonia, and Egypt.[21]

The twenty-three red setting suns in *Color-study watercolor paintings* recall the forty-four sunsets of Antoine de Saint-Exupéry's *Little Prince*, but they also beckon other utopian little-planet islands: the adolescent love island of Île de France, as imagined by the early naturalist Jacques-Henri Bernardin de Saint-Pierre; Daniel Defoe's *Robinson Crusoe*; J.M. Barrie's Neverland; Johann David Wyss's (now Disneyfied) *Swiss Family Robinson*; and, of course, More's famed *Utopia*.

The Waldorf emphasis on fairy tales and imagination provides the *mise-en-scène* not only for keeping imagination alive, but also for learning to read and write through imagination. Children learn to read and write slowly in a Waldorf school. Writing is introduced by

18. Zipes, "Introduction," *Op. cit.*, p. xxxiii. Here, as Zipes points out, Bloch specifically reutilizes a Nazi term, turning it inside out.
19. Bloch, "Better Castles in the Sky," *Op. cit.*, p. 186.
20. Carlgren, *Education towards Freedom*, *Op. cit.*, p. 79.
21. This according to the curriculum as described by Carlgren in *Education towards Freedom*, Ibid., p. 80. Obviously the structure and emphasis varies from school to school, but this is the standard and utilized framework.

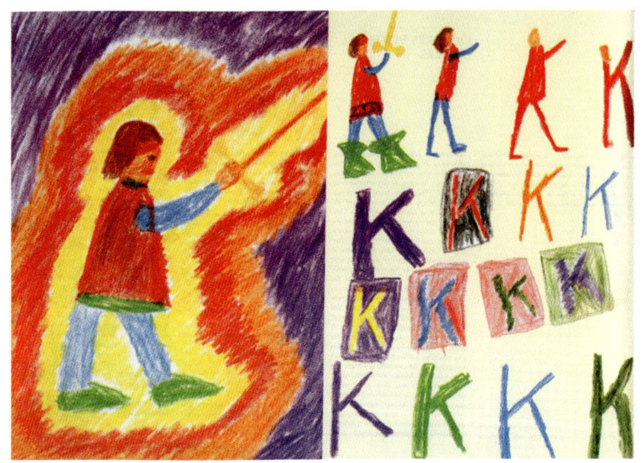

Child's drawing from Frans Carlgren, *Education towards Freedom,* (Sussex, UK: Lanthorn Press, 1981). Courtesy Rudolf Steiner Verlag.

turning pictures into letters. Children read a fairy tale and learn to pronounce the "k" sound of the king who raises his sword. With time, the king eventually metamorphosizes into the letter "k." "The Tall Tree with its outspread branches becomes T, the path over the Mountain remains as the letter M."[22] Only in Grade Two (when the child is about seven years old) is reading taught in a more systematic way, and it is then that "the printed word makes its first appearance."[23]

And just as pictures turn into letters, the sounds of letters turn into bodily expressions with the introduction of eurythmy into the kindergarten class. Steiner believed that "when we speak, a sound is accompanied by a kind of invisible gesture within us. It is this gesture which finds expression in the movements of eurythmy."[24] Under eurythmic instruction, Waldorf students move in response to poems, music, and stories, performing "visible speech" and "visible song."[25] "Pure vowels are often the expression of inner feelings. Ah!, Oh!, Ow!, etc. Words with strongly accented consonants imitate happenings in the world outside, for example, rumble, clatter, whistle, rustle."[26]

22. Ibid., p. 81.
23. Ibid., p. 81.
24. Ibid., p. 56.
25. Ibid., p. 56.
26. Ibid., p. 56.

"O"

A feeling for the sound of "o" circulates within the body of *Threefold Sun*. For not only is the title round once, round twice, round thrice, but there is also an emphasis on going round, in finding the round, and living the round. Round *Gnome houses*—a round ball, unseen, in *Teacher retrieves ball stuck on roof*—the round(ish) puddle in *Mop water used for irrigation*—round, red *Color-study* planets—round the *Maypole in January*—round metal tubs hanging neatly on the wall in *Cleaning supplies*, with raised circles within circles, like a target, like the rings of a cut sequoia whose concentric lines measure the age of a tree—tree stumps as seats in an *Earthen play hut*—*Red balls on roof*—round *Kitchen table* with a red-and-white-checked tablecloth—the ball in *Deflated ball and tree* that wishes to be round. Roundness is the image of utopia, because it is the image of life itself: the earth, the moon, the sun, the pregnant belly, a bird's nest, a marble, a ball, an egg, bowls and cups for food, vases for flowers (like those round vessels in *Kitchen table*). As the phenomenologist Gaston Bachelard insists: life is round. It just is. Roundness is the essence of life: "images of *full roundness* help us to collect ourselves, permit us to confer an initial constitution on ourselves, and to confirm our being intimately inside . . . being cannot be otherwise than round."[27] In a "round cry of round," Bachelard insists that roundness is being, "like a walnut that becomes round in its shell."[28]

Inside the empty *Eurythmy room*, I hear and I feel a round "oh."

utOpia

My concept of utOpia works on the highly theoretical play, the continual movement, of the term as spun out by the great utopian writer Louis Marin (1931–1992) in

27. Gaston Bachelard, *The Poetics of Space*, trans. Maria Jolas. Boston: Beacon Press, 1994, p. 234. First published in French as *La poétique de l'espace*. Paris: Presses Universitaires de France, 1958.
28. Ibid., p. 234.

his *Utopics: The Semiological Play of Textual Spaces*. Like a ship between two shores (perhaps from this world to that island we call Utopia), Marin's utopic discourse is a running back and forth between cultural oppositions, which are always on the move. Marin's utopia is always already contradictory (utopia meets dystopia) and always unfinished.

In *Deflated ball and tree*, dystopic feelings of loss and hopelessness are tagged by the tree, whose roots and life are held in the cement, and by the ball, which is no longer round. This makes the utopic work more real. The fact that Forer does not smooth over the ugly in his move towards utopia, the fact that he is willing to document the less than ideal, makes the warm "voice" of *Threefold Sun* more reliable. *Mop water used for irrigation* is, at first, ugly, but the fact that the water is being reused with ecological awareness makes it becomingly beautiful. While hopeful, this body of photographs acknowledges that it speaks amidst a world in which there is work to be done, a world that is cold, a world that suffers from a lack of productive play, a world frozen by the heft of everyday life, consumer culture, global warming, poverty, racism, soullessness. Speaking specifically to the need to live a creative eco-conscious life, *Threefold Sun*, always setting only to rise again, is work (always already unfinished) working towards the hope of utopia.

Eu-topia

This concept of unfinished work may sound dystopic, but in the hands of some utopian thinkers (like Steiner, Bloch, Marin, even More) this is labor at its happiest. Hellenists now, as in 1516 when More first coined the term "utopia" as both the subject and title of his little book, understand that the word is a fusion of the Greek adverb *ou* (not) and the noun *topos* (place). The etymology of utopia is "not a place." Yet Hellenists also understand utopia "as a punning on the Greek compound, *eutopia*—'happy' or 'fortunate' place."[29] Utopia, then, is at once "not a place" and a "happy place." This confusion, however, is in keeping with More's book. As readers of *Utopia* know, even upon reaching the island of Utopia (as recounted by the narrator-explorer, whose name, Hythloday, turns out to be "another Greek compound that signifies 'nonsense peddler'"[30]), one feels quite perplexed. *Utopia* does not feel like utopia. All leisure activities are sanctioned. There are slaves. Dress is controlled. In fact, the "elaborate constraints imposed on its inhabitants" remind us "of totalitarian regimes."[31] Are we, then, in *eu-topia* or *ou-topia*? The answer would be both. For, More's invention of a "flawed commonwealth"[32] enables us to always see the need for keeping material in flux, always in the process of reconsideration. (Your utopia is not my utopia.) Utopia must always be a never-ending, ever-after making, always enlightened by hope.

Fredric Jameson likens the unfinished work towards utopia as being not unlike the "pleasures of construction" found in "the garage workshop, of the home mechanic erector sets, of Lego, of bricolating and cobbling together things of all kinds . . . in a never-ending variation fed by new ideas and information." For Jameson, "these utopian constructions convey the spirit of non-alienated labor and of production far better than any concepts of *écriture* or *Spiel*"[33] (French or German theoretical, utopian playwriting).

Chalk

Perhaps, then, it is best to inscribe the lessons of utopia in less permeable, light-writing materials, like the intensely colored sticks of well used chalk in *Main Lesson blackboard*. These bits of color are barely visible, but exciting for their potential: like the first heliotropes

29. Logan and Adams, "Introduction," *Op. cit.*, p. xi.
30. Ibid., p. xi.
31. Ibid., p. xii.
32. Ibid., p. xii.
33. Fredric Jameson, "The Politics of Utopia," *New Left Review*, 25, January–February 2004, p. 41.

when winter turns to spring; like the surprise of red camellias in winter; like a hothouse yellow tulip before spring. (Don't miss the bright ray of light that comes from the unseen window and penetrates the violet-colored cloth that absorbs this radiance as if it were a flower drinking in the new sun.)

Steiner's enigmatic lectures were famous for their pictures, charts, abstractions, and words: in sum for their "art." Steiner's influence, including that of his incredible chalkboard technique (the use of colored chalks on black paper, examples of which have been saved by his devotees), is palpable in the work of the great utopian avant-garde German artist Joseph Beuys (1921–1986). Beuys's work took him not only to the chalkboard for his own charismatic lectures, but also to felt, fat, earth, dead animals, copper, iron, blood, chocolate,

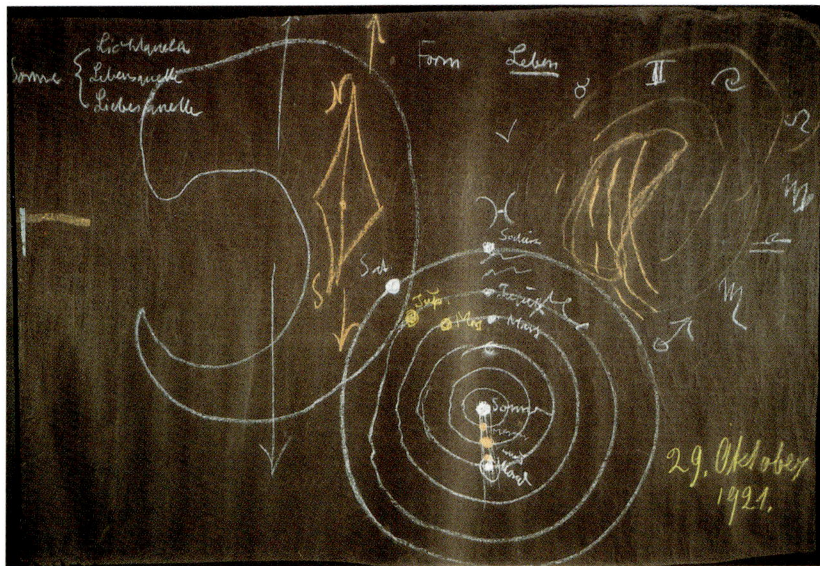

Chalkboard drawing *Threefold Sun* by Rudolf Steiner, Rudolf Steiner, *Blackboard Drawings 1919–1924*, Edited by Walter Kugler, (London: Rudolf Steiner Press, 2003). Courtesy Rudolf Steiner Verlag.

horns, bones, conversation, sound, movement, and honey. As "agitator for social change," Beuys was "active in politics, campaigning for educational reform, grassroots democracy and the Green Party."[34] In 1982, he initiated the planting of seven thousand oak trees, in order to begin to nurse the landscape back to health. The gesture was reparative work, with the future at hand. At his death, Beuys's library contained some one hundred and twenty volumes by Steiner, "thirty some of which were extensively marked with underlining and marginal drawings."[35] Steiner himself made the point that "all real philosophers have been artists in the realm of concepts."[36] Chalk, it seems, is the perfect medium for utopian artists. Never finished, a chalk drawing holds still perceptible traces of former stories, beneath today's stories, with the anticipation of future stories, only an erasure away.

In *We help each other and use kind words*, the two symmetrical chalkboards are at play with one another. On one chalkboard are the rules for keeping a classroom orderly and quiet. These rules would be read differently by the student than they would by the teacher. Yet, utopia cannot be anarchic. Some of us may object to standing quietly and facing forward. Do we really have to raise our hands before speaking? What does it mean to say that "everyone does the best they can"? Do we do our best at our own individual work, or do we do our best within our group as a whole?

We help each other and use kind words interests me because the two texts on two separate boards, with the peeking-in of the cheeky red chair in between, represents in beautiful simplicity the contradictions of utopia. *Alice-in-Wonderland*-like, we have rules that can be read as pertinent *and* absurd, alongside the wishes for white rabbits, here in two trios. Socialist at heart, the purchase of these two sets of three-fold rabbits will be made through the equal contributions of each member of the class. These rabbits, alive and so full of anticipation, hail *Two deer three raccoons* (the raccoons and deer buried to enrich the soil and give new life).

---

34. "Introduction" to the Tate Modern booklet that accompanied the exhibition, *Joseph Beuys, February 4–May 2, 2005*, unpaginated, no author listed.
35. David Adams, "From Queen Bee to Social Sculpture: The Artistic Alchemy of Joseph Beuys (1921–1986)," in Rudolf Steiner, *Bees*, trans. Thomas Braatz. Hudson, New York: Anthroposophic Press, 1998, p. 193.
36. Rudolf Steiner, *The Philosophy of Spiritual Activity*, trans. Rita Stebbing. 1894; reprint, London: Rudolf Steiner Press, 1992, p. 177.

Utopia: Light and Dark

We are drawn to Utopia today, now that "utopia" has recovered from being a cold war synonym for Stalinism (with its ties to enforced uniformity, neglect of human frailty, and perfection achieved through force), now that "capitalism seems to have no natural enemies."[37] As Jameson sadly comments on the force of capitalism today:

> It is not only the invincible universality of capitalism which is at issue: tirelessly undoing the social gains made since the inception of the socialist and communist movements, repealing all the welfare measures, the safety net, the right to unionization, industrial and ecological regulatory laws, offering to private pensions and indeed to dismantle whatever stands in the way of the free market all over the world. What is crippling is not the presence of an enemy, but rather the universal belief, not only that this tendency is irreversible, but that the historic alternatives to capitalism have been proven unviable and impossible, and that no other socio-economic system is conceivable, let alone practically available.[38]

Nevertheless, it is important to understand that our concept of utopia emerges not only from and in response to both the formative and late periods of Western capitalism, but also alongside the development of Judeo-Christian "enlightened" nationhood.[39] In Steiner's strongly German-centered anthroposophy, we often see this moving towards a theological light that is too close for comfort to the frightening shimmer of the Third Reich. Can one simply overlook the coupling of Steiner's Christianity with stories of evolved purity? Steiner's inspiring parts are cut by an ugliness, a truth that Forer embraces in the not-so-beautiful parts of *Threefold Sun*.

I wonder at the significance of the one picture—*Waldorf high school cover-band member's car, Valentine's Day*—that seems to stand apart in this organism called

---

37. Fredric Jameson, *Archaeologies of the Future: The Desire Called Utopia and Other Science Fictions*. London and New York: Verso, 2005, pp. xi–xii.
38. Ibid., p. xii.
39. From conversation with Professor Ranji Khanna, Duke University. Between the years 2002 and 2005, I was in a writing group with Professor Khanna and I shall always be indebted to the insights that she shared with me over those years.

Threefold Sun. I know that the car, the very metonym of Los Angeles itself, is at the heart of global warming, bad labor practices, too-fast life, too-material life, teenagers on the go, and not enough time at home. The car is a Mercedes-Benz and it belongs to a student at this Los Angeles Waldorf school. The sheet is a cover-up of what? Car culture? Elitism? A connection to a Nazi past? Or is it revealing the covering up of the darkness of American history? The whiteness and class specificity of a Waldorf education? What? What kind of shroud is it? Perhaps this is just the kind of material thought that Forer desires to wrap us into.

In an inversion of Steiner's Christian-based spirituality, we find Bloch's discourse on hope, written from the position of a Jewish, atheist theologian. Bloch despised Steiner's work and wrote in *Heritage of Our Times* (1935) that he regarded parts of the anthroposophist movement as a "fascist reaction,"[40] labeling the movement in *The Principle of Hope* as "cobbled together myth-cosmology" (Bloch III, 1187). Bloch understood Steiner as a "second-rate: clairvoyant" (Bloch III, 1186).[41] Relentless in his criticism, Bloch writes: "Steiner reigns, gossipy and quarter educated . . . [His work is] at every point atavistic spookiness, trivialized astral myth, travestied 'natural science.'"[42] (Nevertheless Bloch does find a tiny bit of light, suggesting that someone with "an advanced consciousness which is well disposed to colportage" might be able to find a glimmer of hope in Steiner's work.[43]) Steiner and Bloch, both German, were revered and criticized equally for their religious mysticism. To take up these two utopianists—Steiner, the unwitting proponent of the fascism of prewar Germany, and Bloch, the suffering Jew who lived through the horrors of Hitler's regime—is to utopically engage oppositions, a theoretical approach driven by Marin's discourse (negative, yet driven by hope).

In the poetic words of Emily Dickinson: "'Hope' is the thing with feathers / That perches in the soul."[44]

---

40. Ernst Bloch, *Heritage of our Times*, trans. Neville Plaice and Stephen Plaice. Berkeley: University of California Press, 1991, p. 170.
41. As Bloch writes in *The Principle of Hope*, Op. cit., 3:1186–87: "And let us not forget what second-rate clairvoyance achieves here . . . At the peak of 'Knowledge of Higher Worlds' the occult journalist Rudolf Steiner established himself, a mediocrity in his own right. A mediocre, indeed unbearable curiosity, yet effective, as if mistletoe were still being broken off here, as if something shoddily druidical were fermenting, soaking, murmuring and chattering on newspaper. Whether the chatter and the low level are necessary for this kind of 'initiation' or occult activation it is difficult to say. There are a few, a very few, serious writings from the Steiner circle."
42. Bloch, *Heritage of Our Times*, Op. cit., p. 174.
43. Ibid., p. 176.
44. Emily Dickinson, *The Complete Poems of Emily Dickinson*, ed. Thomas H. Johnson. London: Little, Brown & Company, 1961, p. 116. The poem was written around 1861.

Marin enables me to mix *Threefold Sun* three times over (Forer, Steiner, and Bloch) in order to restore play between the cog and the wheel: the play of time (past and future, dead and alive, new world and old world), the play of labor (affected and disembodied, agrarian and capitalism), the play of geography (Germany, the United States, real places, and mythological places). Alone, each of these three texts (the photographs of *Threefold Sun*, Steiner's anthroposophy, Bloch's illuminating *Vor-Schein*) may or may not work like a projection of utopia as ideological critique, but the meta-discourse that the Marinesian lens affords does: it stages utopic play between the spaces of Forer, Steiner, and Bloch and delivers me to a place that might be called Waldorf school or biodynamic farming or the mere simplicity of eurythmic movement. It might *just* be listening to a fairy tale at dusk or painting something red.

I See Red

Blood is red.
Passion is red.

Steiner writes: "When we meet a woman in a red dress, we experience her as inauthentic, if she is too modest."[45]

Love is red, like a valentine.
Roses are red.
Courage is red.
Rage is red.
Little Red Riding Hood is red.
Red is precious.

---

45. Rudolf Steiner, "Impressionism and Expressionism," in Michael Howard, ed., *Art as Spiritual Activity, Rudolf Steiner's Contribution to the Visual Arts*. Hudson, New York: Anthroposophic Press, 1998, p. 197.

Garnets are red.

Joy is red.

In ancient alchemy, red denotes final attainment of the philosopher's stone, enabling the transformation of lead into gold.

The moon can appear red.

A bull cannot bear the sight of red.

In sac*red* and marty*red*, I see red.

In a black and white darkroom, the photographer works under the light of a red bulb.

Red appears with great frequency in *Threefold Sun*.

We see red in the form of cheeky little fragments. It is crusty in *Boy with bloody nose*. It is neat in *Cleaning supplies*. It is comfy on Ekkehard Heyder, a beloved German-born Waldorf teacher, now retired, from Forer's own school days. It is curious on the one teenager in *Practical arts class meeting* who wears a red hoodie, while his peers are mostly in blues and greens.

In the row of red planets in *Color-study watercolor paintings*, which fill me with red joy, I am soaked in red Rothko plenitude. *I am proud we are human* is made of messy reds: dirty red, brick red, clay red, and the red sienna of my childhood crayons. Red even turns into a ghastly pink in the painted bricks of *Teacher's desk*. The bold Mexican rainbow serape makes the pink just that much more pink. As an adolescent, I would have loved this pink, this office with its wooly white lambskin covered chair: it would have made a place for me. In *Waiting for mom after school*, I am striped with the red of dried blood by the bench and the boy's shirt, exactly the same color as the round solid drops, which still must be there, on the cement sidewalk near my childhood home, where I once took a terrible fall. Lines and drops that I used to step over every day on my way home from school: "Step on a line and break your mother's spine."

Although it took time for me to notice it, once found, I saw red everywhere in *Threefold Sun*.

Metamorphosis

Red, like utopia, is a contradictory color.

Threefold Sun accepts red for all its crisscross anxiousness, as if the color were a spirited child. Understanding red as a color to run towards, but also as a color to turn away from, to turn inside out, to turn back into green, *Threefold Sun* embodies many of the color principles of Steiner and his beloved Goethe. As Goethe writes in "The Metamorphosis of Plants" (1790):

> Researchers have been generally aware for some time that there is a hidden relationship among various external parts of the plant which develop one after the other and, as it were, one out of the other (e.g. leaves, calyx, corolla, and stamens). The process by which one and the same organ appears in a variety of forms [as in a green leaf becoming a red petal] has been called the metamorphosis of plants . . . It can be seen to work step by step from the first seed leaves to the last formation of the fruit.[46]

---

46. Johann Wolfgang von Goethe, *Scientific Studies*, ed. and trans. Douglas Miller. Princeton: Princeton University Press, p. 76. See also, Goethe's poem "Metamorphosis of Plants" (1797).

This theory of Goethe's metamorphosized into Steiner's own green-into-red words:

In my thoughts I look now, for example, upon the rose and say, "In the red rose petal I see the color of the green plant sap transformed into red, and the red rose, like the green leaf, follows the pure, passionless laws of growth."[47]

Steiner understood color like Goethe, whose study of color was scientific, though it revealed vision as subjective, both empirically and as posited by "various 'romanticisms' and early modernisms as the active, autonomous producer of his or her own visual experience."[48] Goethe was particularly struck by colors seen while inside a camera obscura, after the hole is sealed and the viewer is confronted with mysterious afterimages: where colored circles float, undulate, and undergo a "sequence of chromatic transformations, producing 'physiological' colors belonging entirely to the body of the observer and are 'the necessary conditions of vision.'"[49] In other words, Goethe's color theory is explained through what he perceived as scientific and empirical data—but it was also always already cultural and personal. And, for Steiner, the cultural as teamed with the personal can evolve into the coveted spiritual of new attainment: the "threefold sun."

Steiner envisioned the education of the Waldorf student with these poetics of meta-morphosis, which revolve around the ability to use one's hands in the service of a productive mind, just as a string can learn to be a sweater, clay can learn to be a bowl, wood can learn to be a table, a seed can learn to be a cabbage. In a Waldorf school, children are instructed in the arts of handwork, with the idea that this does indeed develop their minds: "In the first class, children begin to knit and in the second class to crochet. Gradually they become able to make garments for themselves or others until by class VII or VIII they can make a shirt, a dress, a pair of trousers etc., with the help of a sewing machine."[50] For Steiner, the ability to use one's hands and fingers is the making of the shell of the soul that protects and cultivates the seed of the intellect, so that the green leaf can turn into the red petal.

47. Rudolf Steiner, *An Outline of Occult Science.* Spring Valley, New York: Anthroposophic Press, 1972, p. 266.
48. Jonathan Crary, *On Vision and Modernity in the Nineteenth Century.* Cambridge, Massachusetts: MIT Press, 1990, p. 69.
49. Ibid., p. 68.
50. Carlgren, *Education towards Freedom, Op. cit.,* p. 49.

I see red.

I feel blue.

The quality of light, morning red, distant blue, the blue hour of twilight,
are metaphorical expressions of states of consciousness, both individual and social,
and states of hope and realization.
Neville Plaice, Stephen Plaice, and Paul Knight (on Bloch)[51]

Steiner, with the aid of Goethe, chose to read his colors as a literal, yet poetic, language: blues and greens are sympathetic colors and reds and yellows are antipathetic colors. They speak. They are inseparable. Of his afterimages, Goethe writes: "No sooner, however, is the whole circle red than the edge begins to be blue, and the blue gradually encroaches on the red."[52] Steiner, too, had very specific feelings that he attached to the colors red and blue:

> If someone invites us into a room with red walls, our assumption about the red walls has to do with artistic perception. When I am led into a red room and face the person who invited me there, it seems natural for that person to tell me all sorts of things that I find valuable and interesting. If this does not happen, I feel that the invitation to the red room was a lie, and I leave unsatisfied. On the other hand, if someone receives me in a blue room and chatters so much that I cannot get a word in edgewise, the whole situation would make me uncomfortable, thinking that this person has conveyed a false impression to me through the very color of the room.[53]

Turn red into blue and you will find yourself inside Giotto's heavenly blue Arena Chapel, staring at the angel in Hell, tearing the blue away, with the sky as scroll, to

51. Plaice, Plaice, and Knight, "Translator's Introduction," *Op. cit.*, p. xxxi.
52. Johann Wolfgang von Goethe, *Theory of Colours*, trans. Charles Eastlake (1840). Cambridge: MIT Press, 1970, p. 17. Also quoted in Crary, *On Vision and Modernity*, *Op. cit.*, p. 68.
53. Steiner, "Impressionism and Expressionism," *Op. cit.*, pp. 196–197.

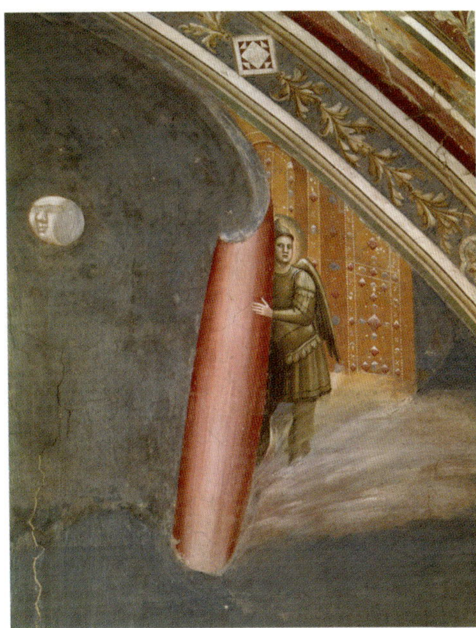

Detail of Angel. Fresco by Giotto
di Bondone (1266–1336).
Arena Chapel, Padua, Italy,
Art Resource.

reveal apocalyptic red. (Goethe and Steiner are right: blue is lined with red). As is so
beautifully written in Isaiah: "All the stars of the heavens will be dissolved and the sky
rolled up like a scroll; all the starry host will fall like withered leaves from the vine,
like shriveled figs from the fig tree" (34: 4). And, likewise, in Revelation we find that
"the whole moon turned blood red, and the stars in the sky fell to earth, as late figs
drop from a fig tree when shaken by a strong wind. The sky receded like a scroll,
rolling up, and every mountain and island was removed from its place" (6: 12–17).[54] In
the land of *Threefold Sun*, a seed grown from the utopian dreams of Steiner, red is a
color that we are called upon to integrate with our more kindhearted and benevolent
blue feelings.

---

54. Both passages are from the *New International Version*. I am indebted to Sarah Miller for guiding me towards these passages.

As Steiner said in his lecture on "Perception of the Elemental World" (1913):

If a being of the elemental world is antipathetic, it means that it has a distinct characteristic of that world which must be described as antipathetic, and we have to deal with it just as we deal in the sense world with the colors blue and red—not permitting one to be more sympathetic to us than the other. Here we meet all the colors with a certain calmness because they convey what the things are; only when a person is a bit neurotic does he run away from certain colors, or when he is a bull and cannot bear the sight of red. Most of us accept all the colors with equanimity and in the same way we should be able to observe with the utmost calmness the qualities of sympathy and antipathy that belong to the elemental world.

Consider, then, Forer's *Maypole*: it stands austere, too overly centered in a cold blanket of snow: without its ribbons, its flowers pop with yellow, pink, purple, and, yes, a bit of cheeky red. A little something cerulean (a tool shed, a refuse container, who knows?) beckons me with a bit of blue hope. The snow and the ribbons torn from the pole, like so many tongues from the mouth, silently speak to me with twofold loss. We see life there in the maypole flowers, purples and reds, which speak monosyllables of joy in the chilled picture. The flowers make us remember the ribbons from the past and anticipate the ribbons of the future. Red, perhaps the most paradoxical of all colors, works like this picturing of life and death.

Forer uses color to speak. His colors tell stories. Colors for Forer (and for Steiner) are not inanimate; they are animistic and have personalities, souls even. Steiner put it this way:

You can speak to the children in the language of colors. Just think how inspiring it is if you give the children to understand: this is a coquettish mauve, and there is a cheeky little bit of red looking over her shoulder; and both of them are standing on a humble blue. You must describe it quite graphically; it is formative for the soul . . . What is thus perceived as arising out of the colors can be put on paper in fifty different ways.[55]

Similarly, Steiner tells us that "an excitable child should be surrounded and even dressed in red and orange colors and in contrast a placid child should be given blues and greenish blues. What is important is the opposite color reproduced inwardly."[56]

In Forer's photograph of a Waldorf eurythmy room, colorful garments in waiting are partially revealed as if hiding underneath the white sheets that cover them, as if they were melancholic blue children or choleric red children or sanguine yellow children or phlegmatic white children, reflected in the shine of the varnished floor.[57] I see in *Eurythmy room* Steiner's color theory held under two *clouds* of white sheets, waiting to be worn, waiting to be eurythmified . . . *eutopia*.

I see red and I feel blue.
I see the *Vor-Schein*.
I am that much closer to home.
I am that much closer to utopia spelled with an "e."
I feel "oh."
Full circle.

I move. From early on we are searching . . .

---

55. Steiner, from a teacher's conference in 1920, as quoted by Carlgren, *Education towards Freedom*, *Op. cit.*, p. 47.
56. Steiner, as quoted by Carlgren, Ibid., p. 46.
57. Scholars of Freud will recognize the image of the antique relief in the background as Gradiva herself: the object of an obsession that turns on how the figure steps out with her particular and beautiful style of walking. See Wilhelm Jensen's *Gradiva* and Freud's *Delusion and Dream*, published together in Freud's *Delusion and Dream*, trans. Helen M. Downey. New York: Mofat, Yard & Company, 1917. As Jensen writes: "the flight-like poise, combined with a firm step, lent her the peculiar grace," (5). The photographer and writer Victor Burgin has long been obsessed with Gradiva in his own work, both in writing and in a photographic project. Most recently he describes Jensen's story as follows: "The novella tells of a young archaeologist who becomes fascinated by an antique relief of a woman stepping forward. The man is obsessed with the question of whether the woman's gait, the particular manner in which she steps out—now immobilized in stone—could have been drawn for life or whether it was entirely the invention of the artist. In the grip of his obsession he searches amongst women who pass in the street for an example of Gradiva's ambulatory manner—but without success. As his obsession approaches delirium his investigations become a quest for Gradiva herself"; see Victor Burgin, *The Remembered Film*.

plates

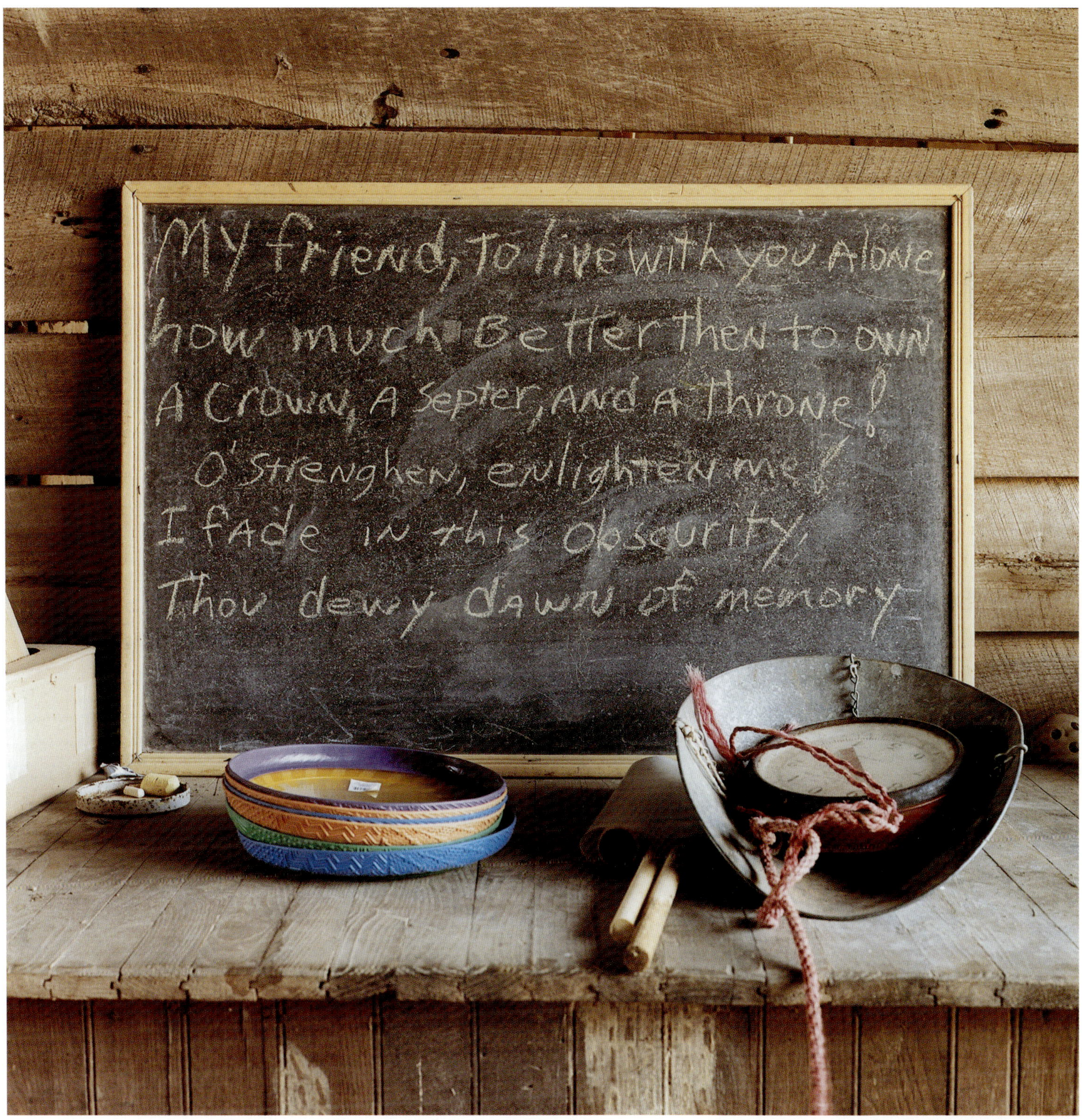
MY friend, To live with you Alone,
how much Better then to own
A Crown, A Septer, And A Throne!
O' strenghen, enlighten me!
I fade in this Obscurity,
Thou dewy dawn of memory

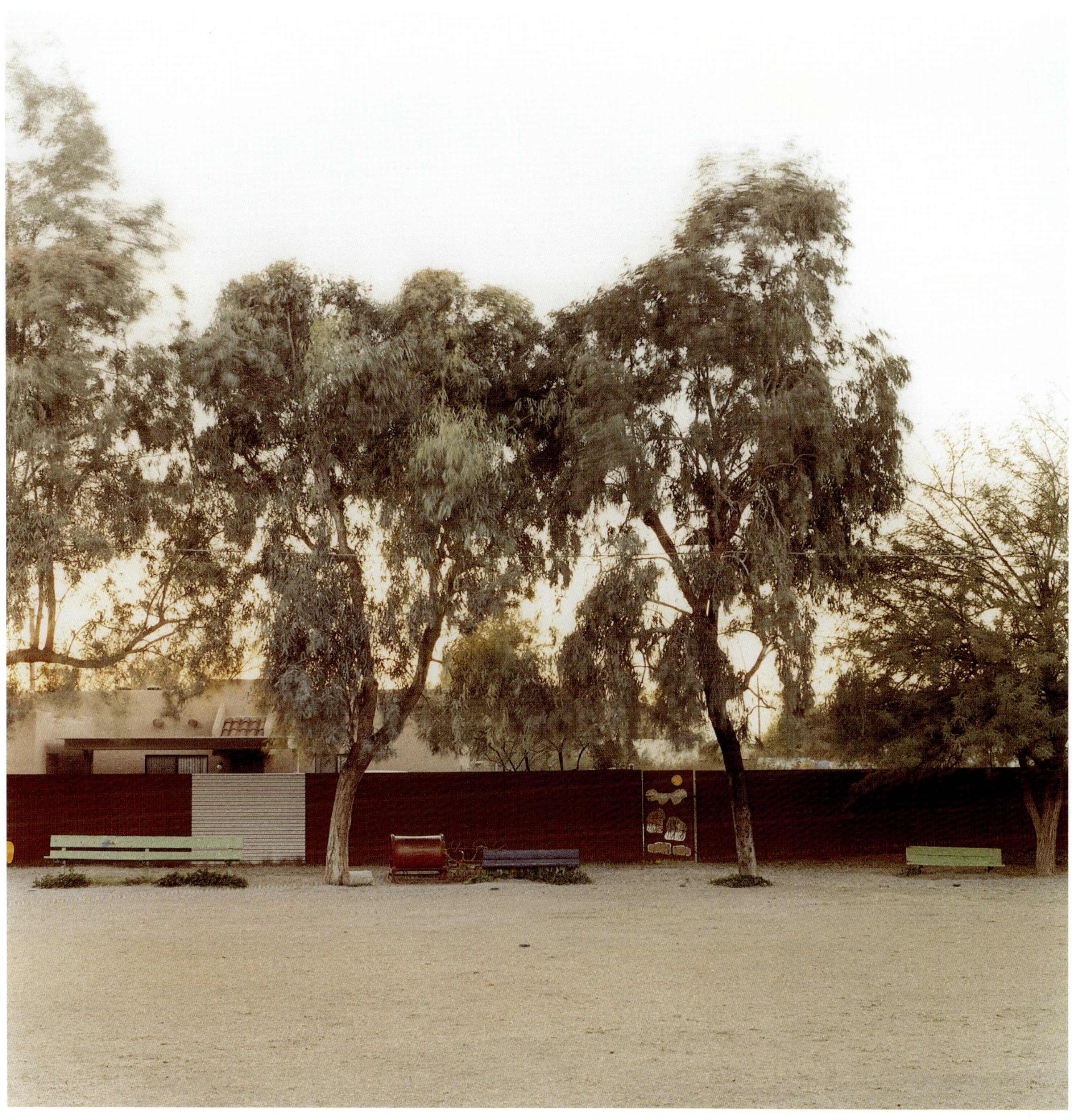

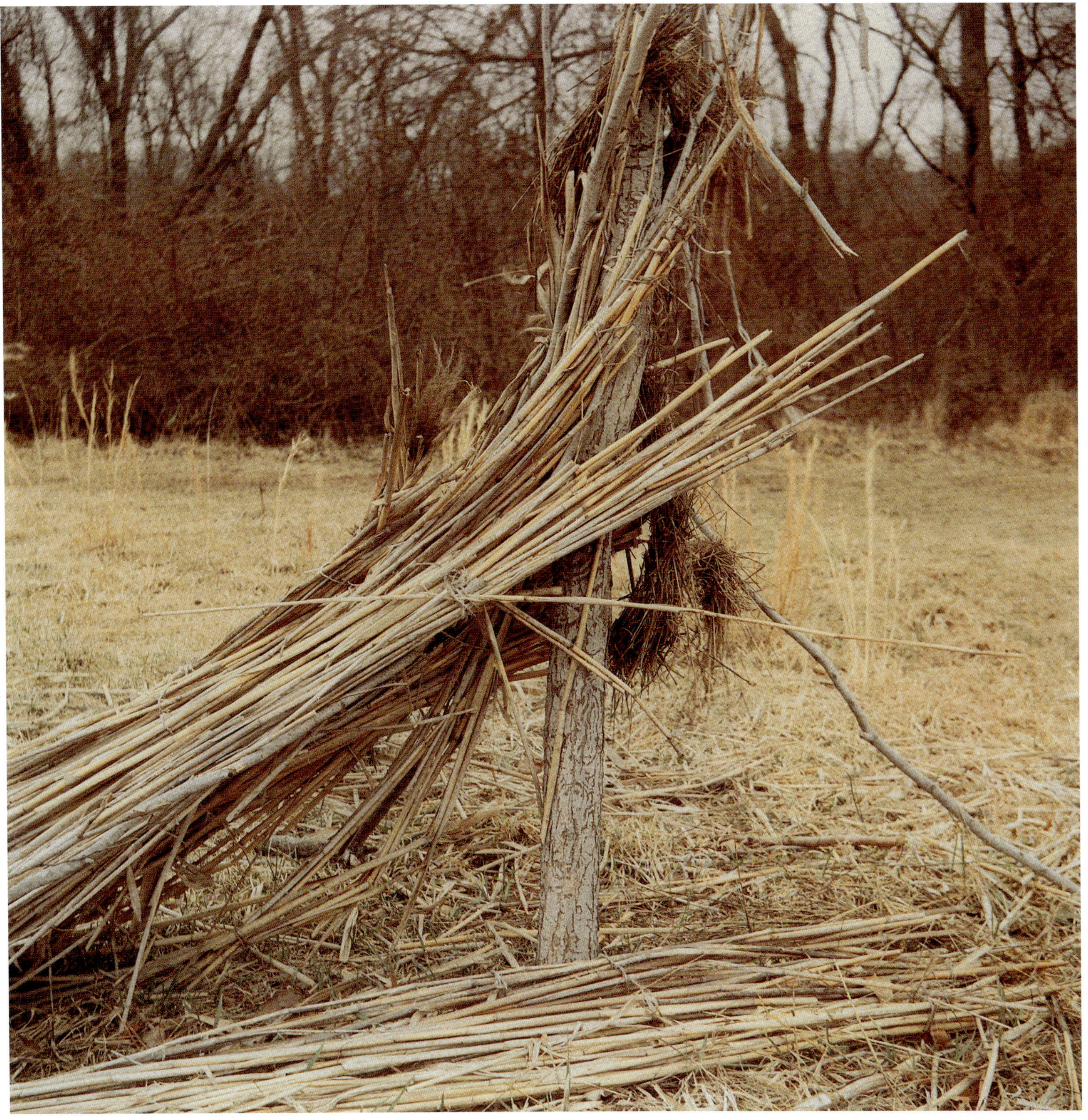

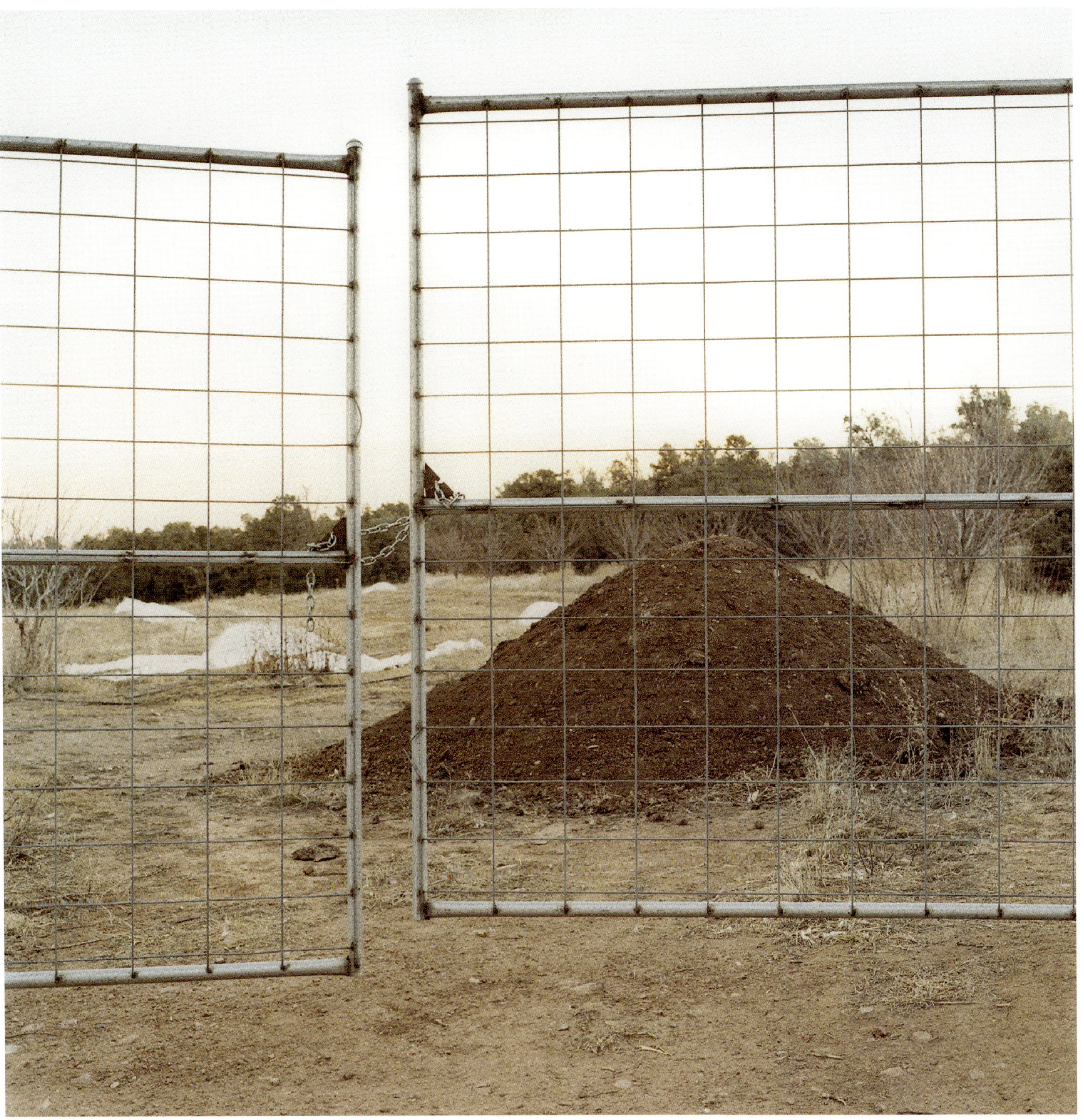

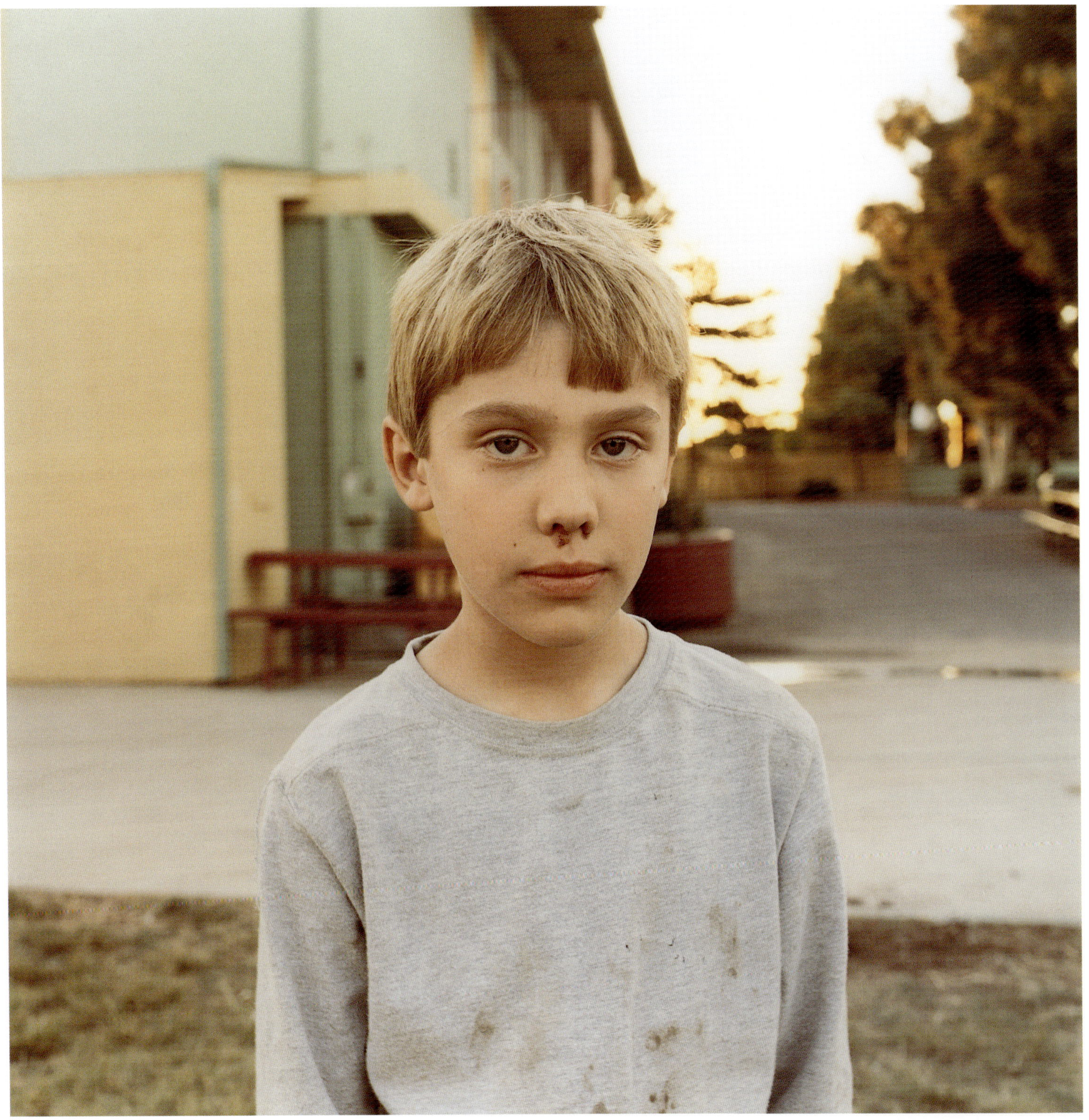

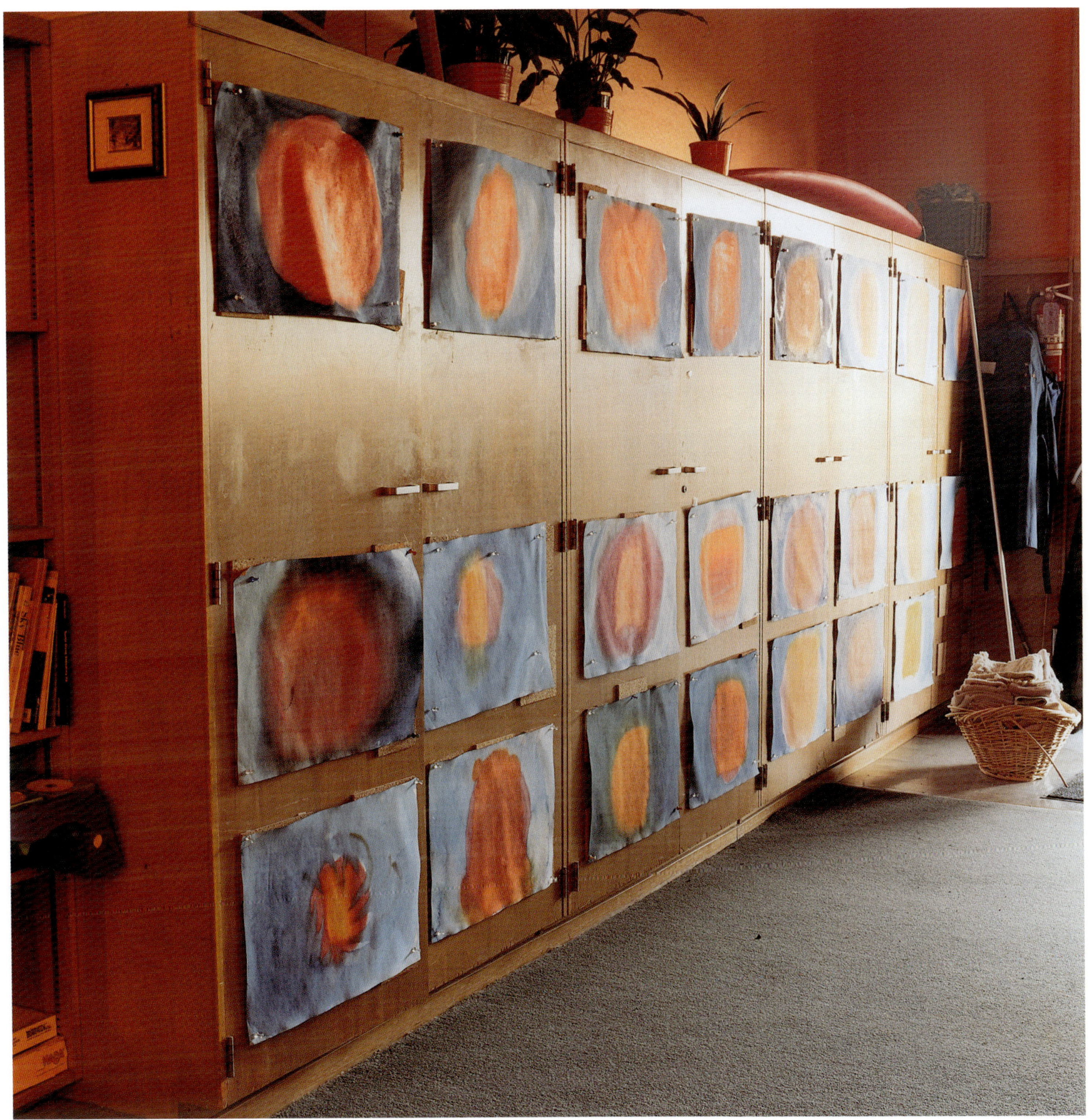

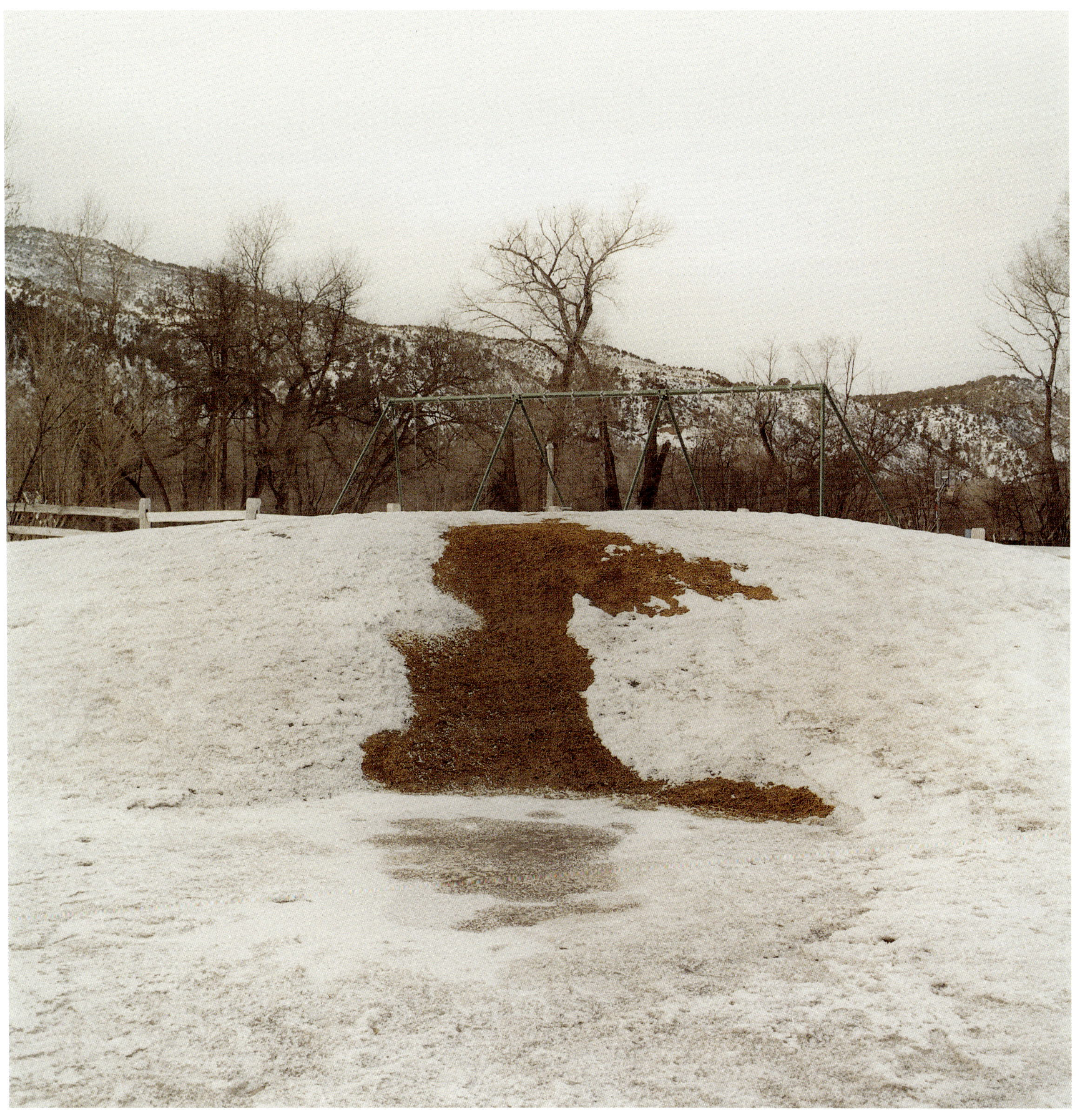

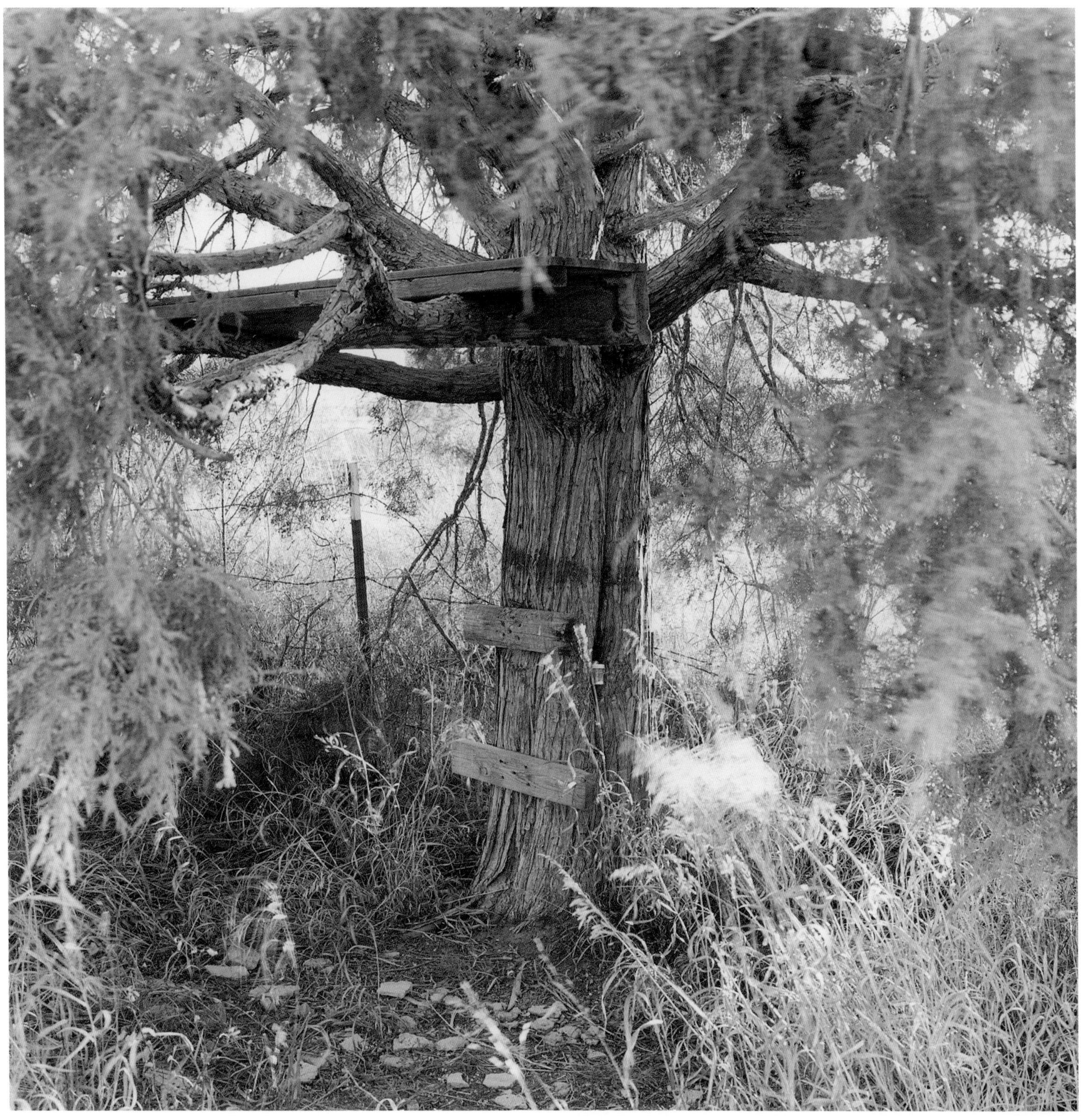

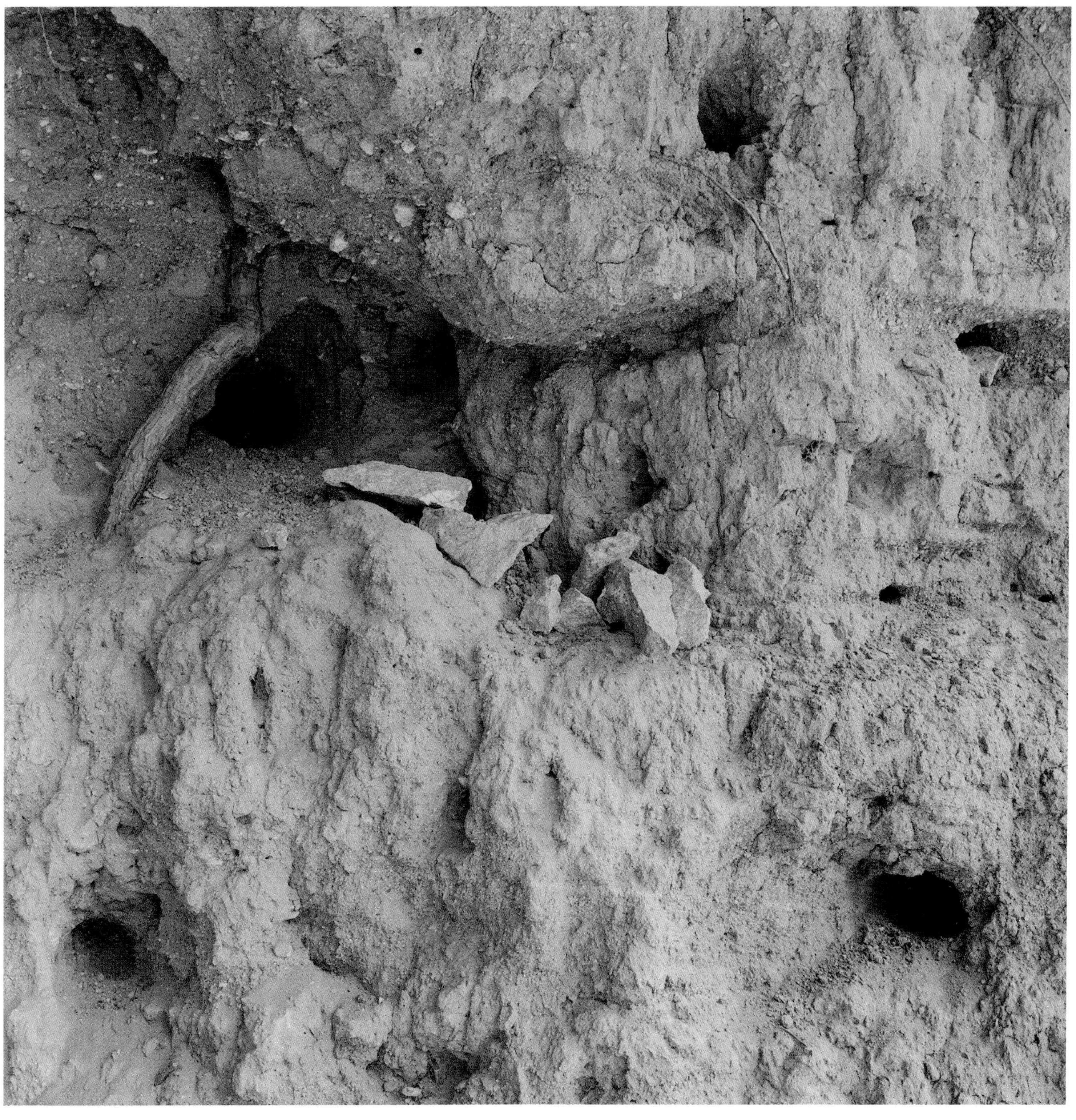

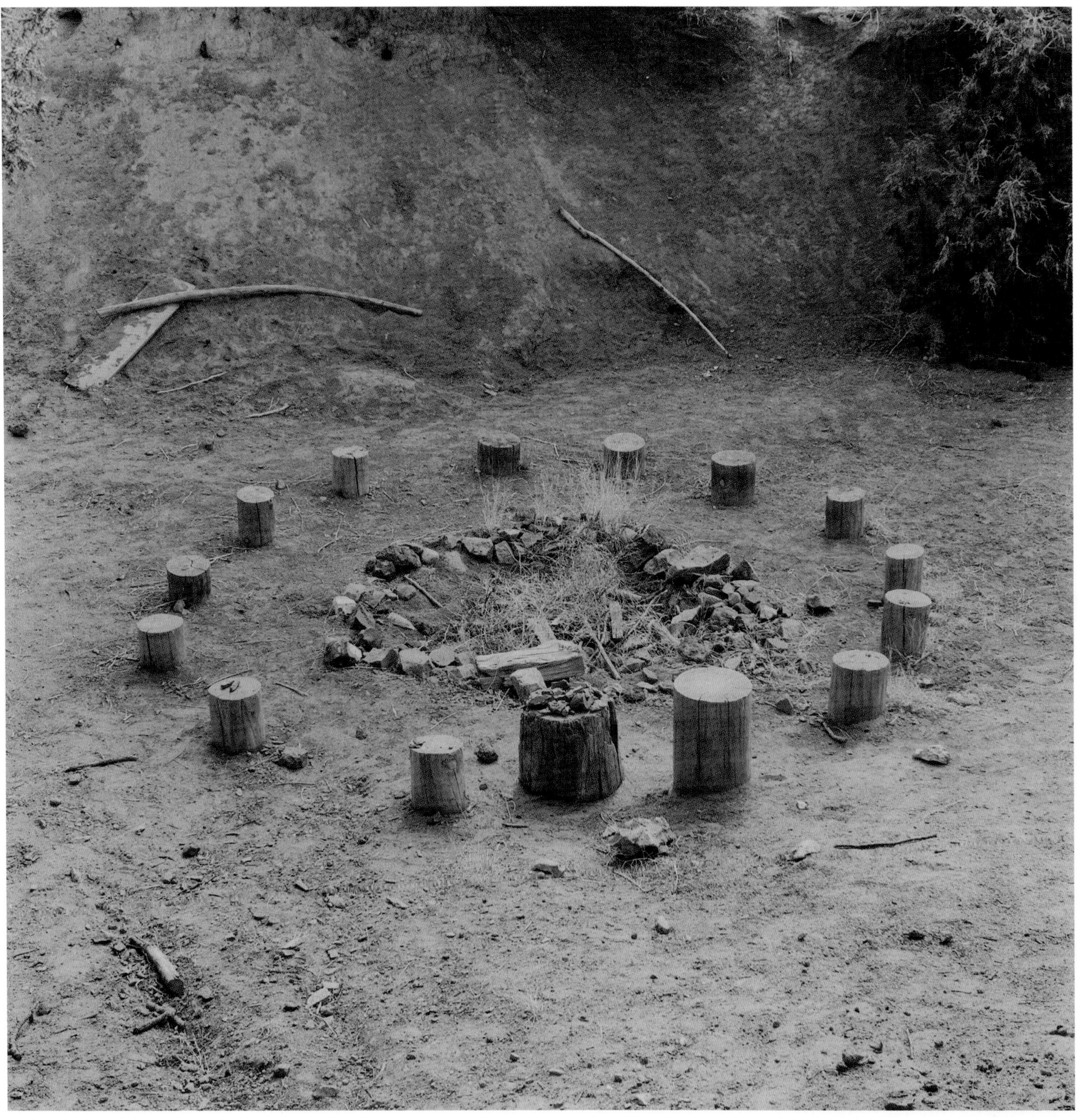

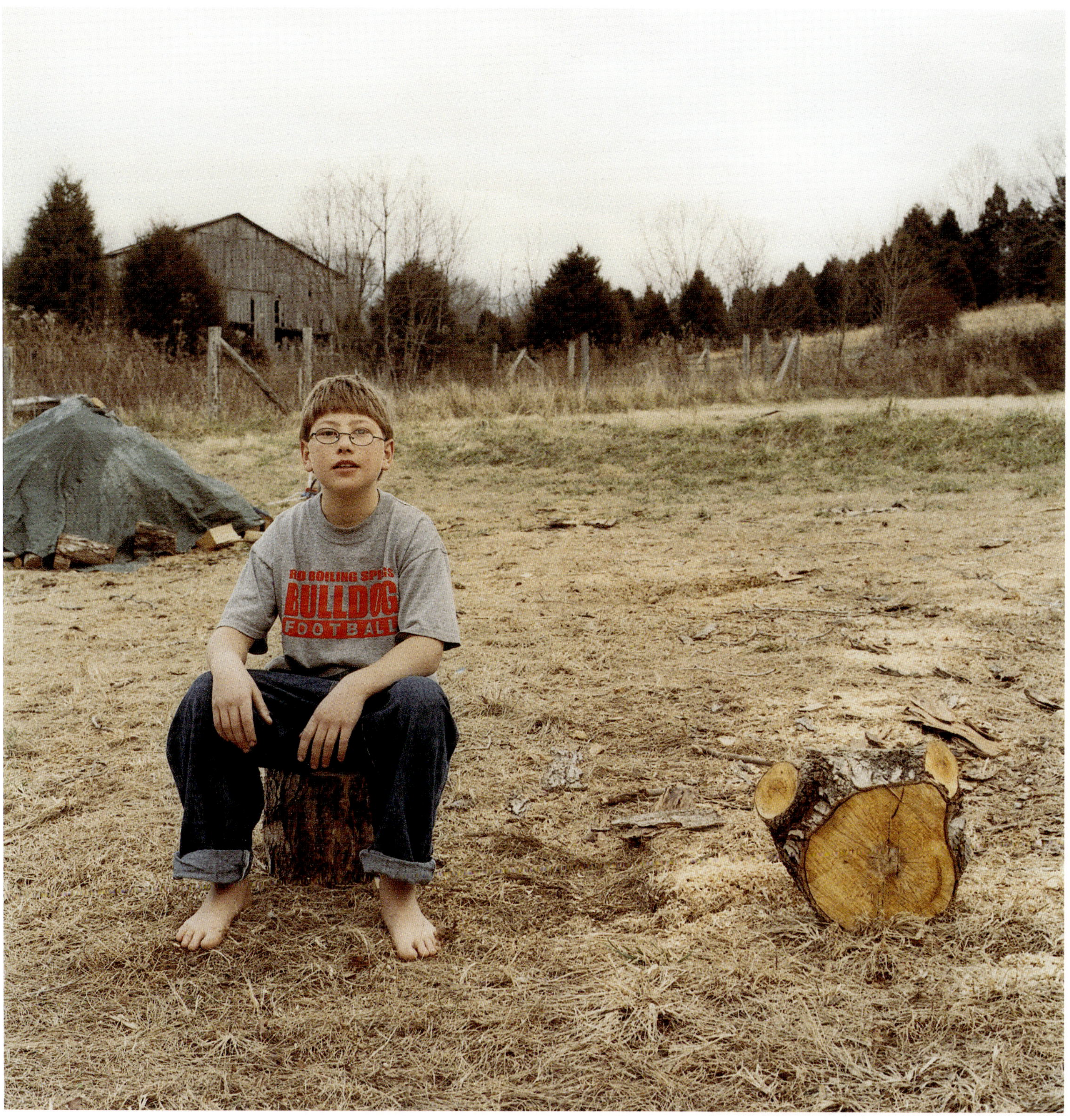

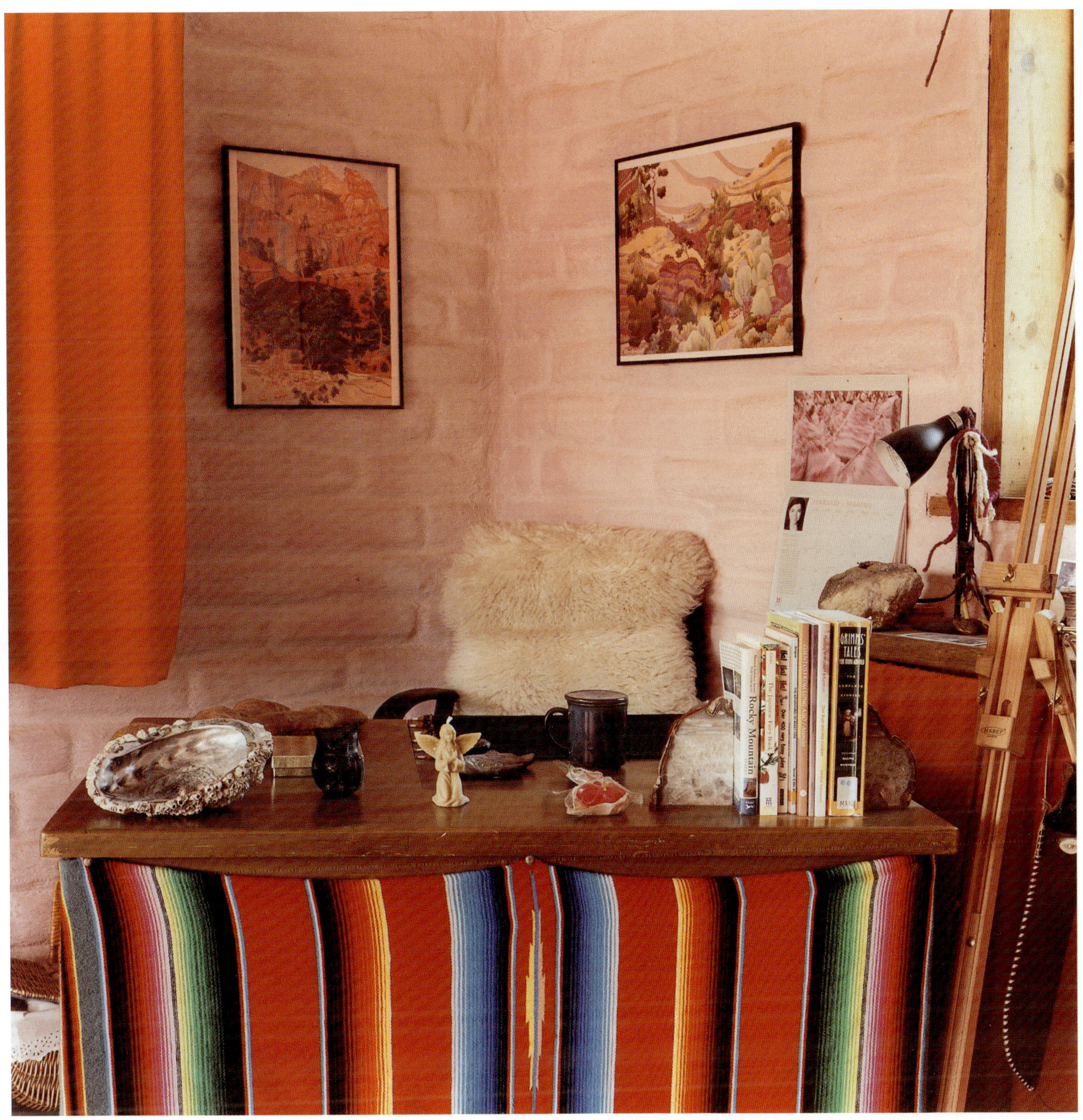

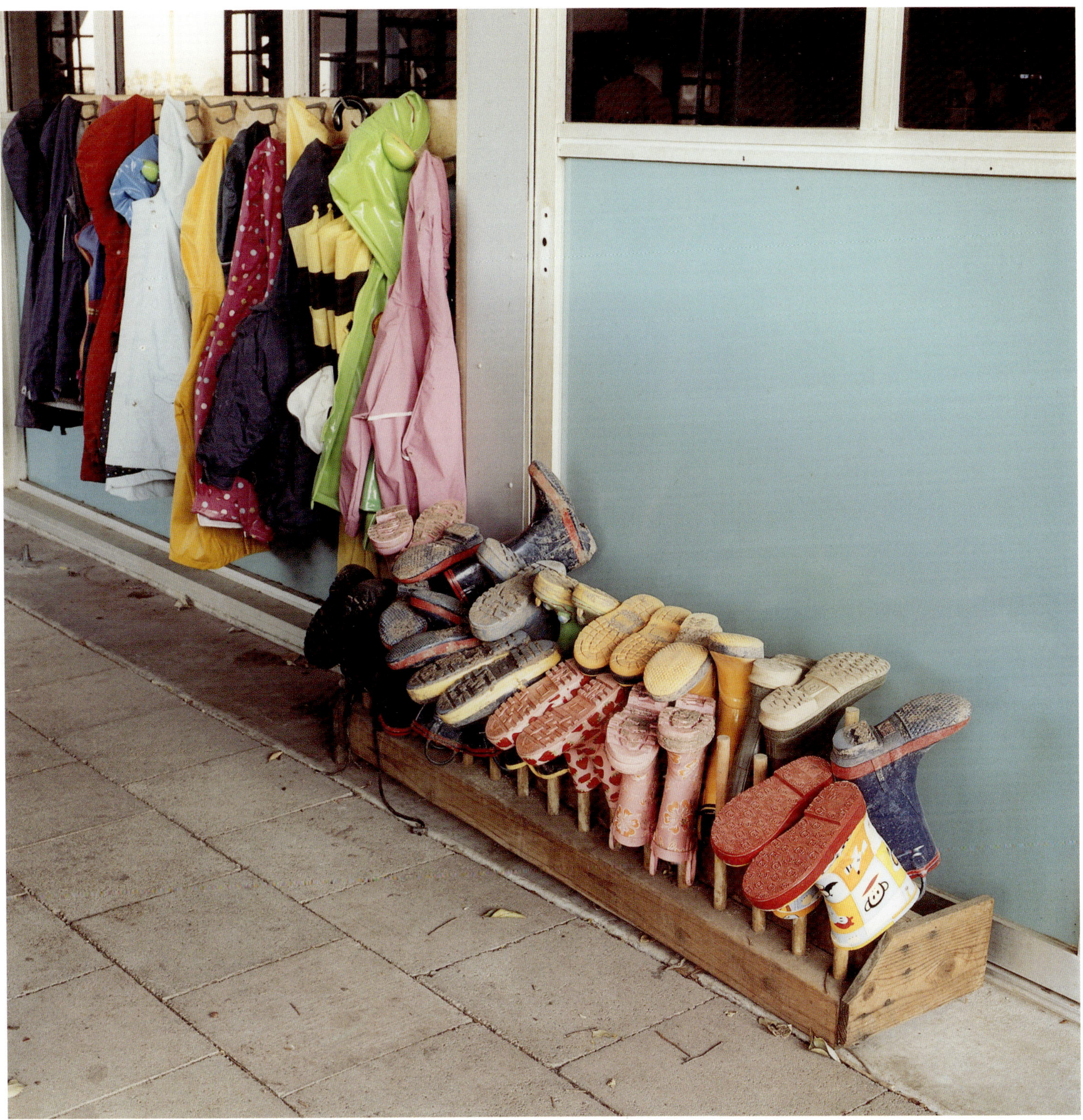

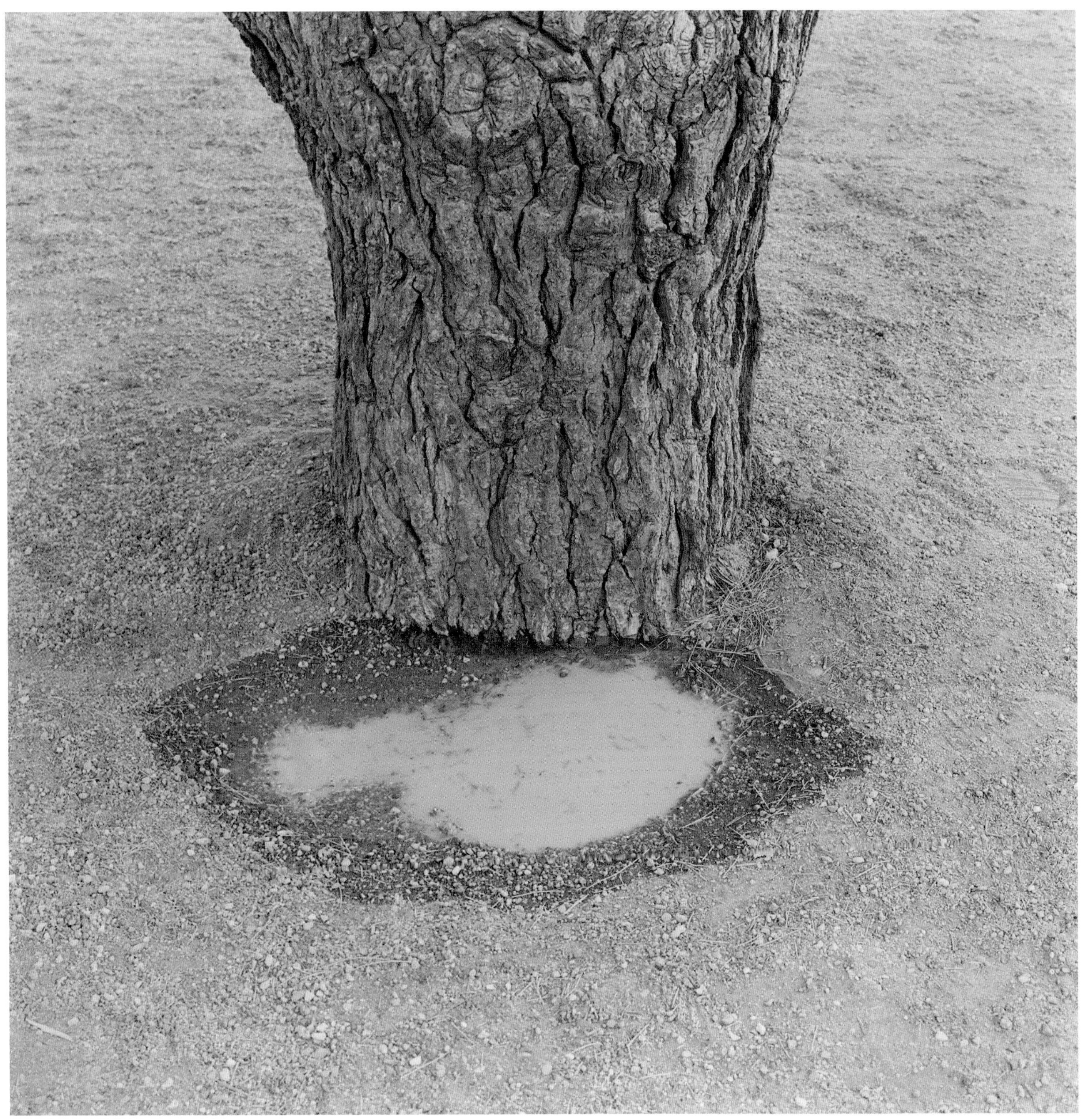

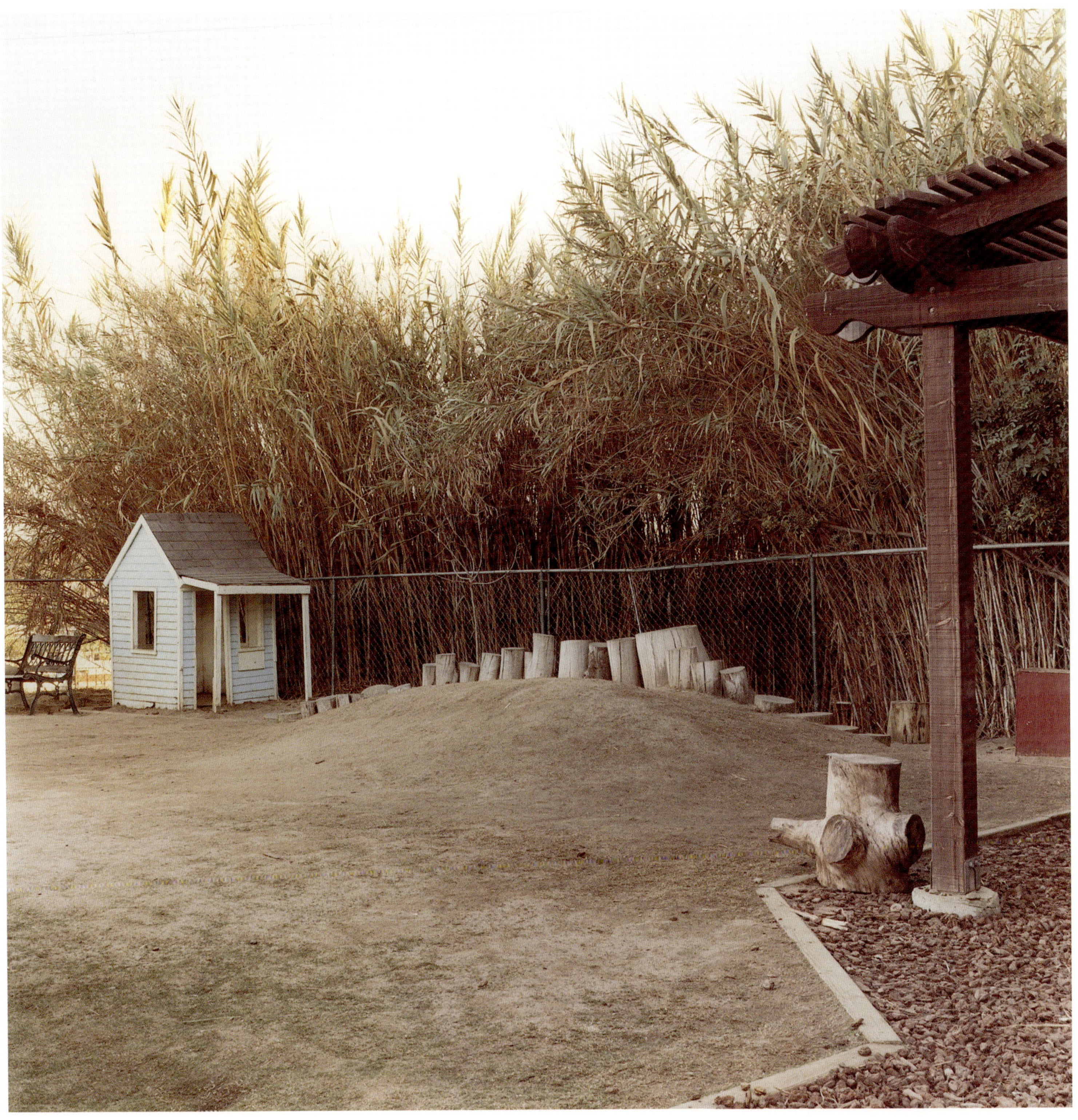

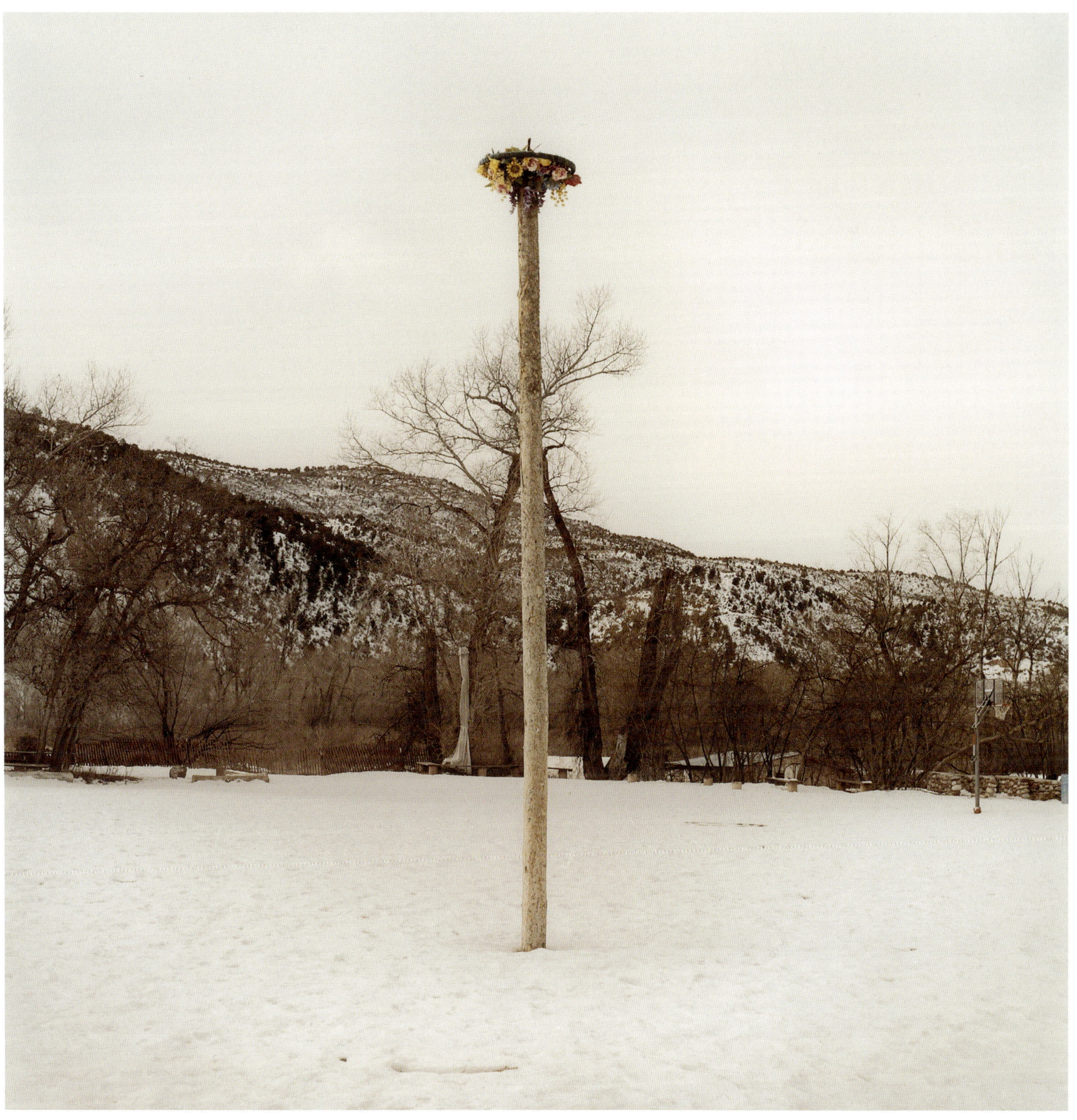

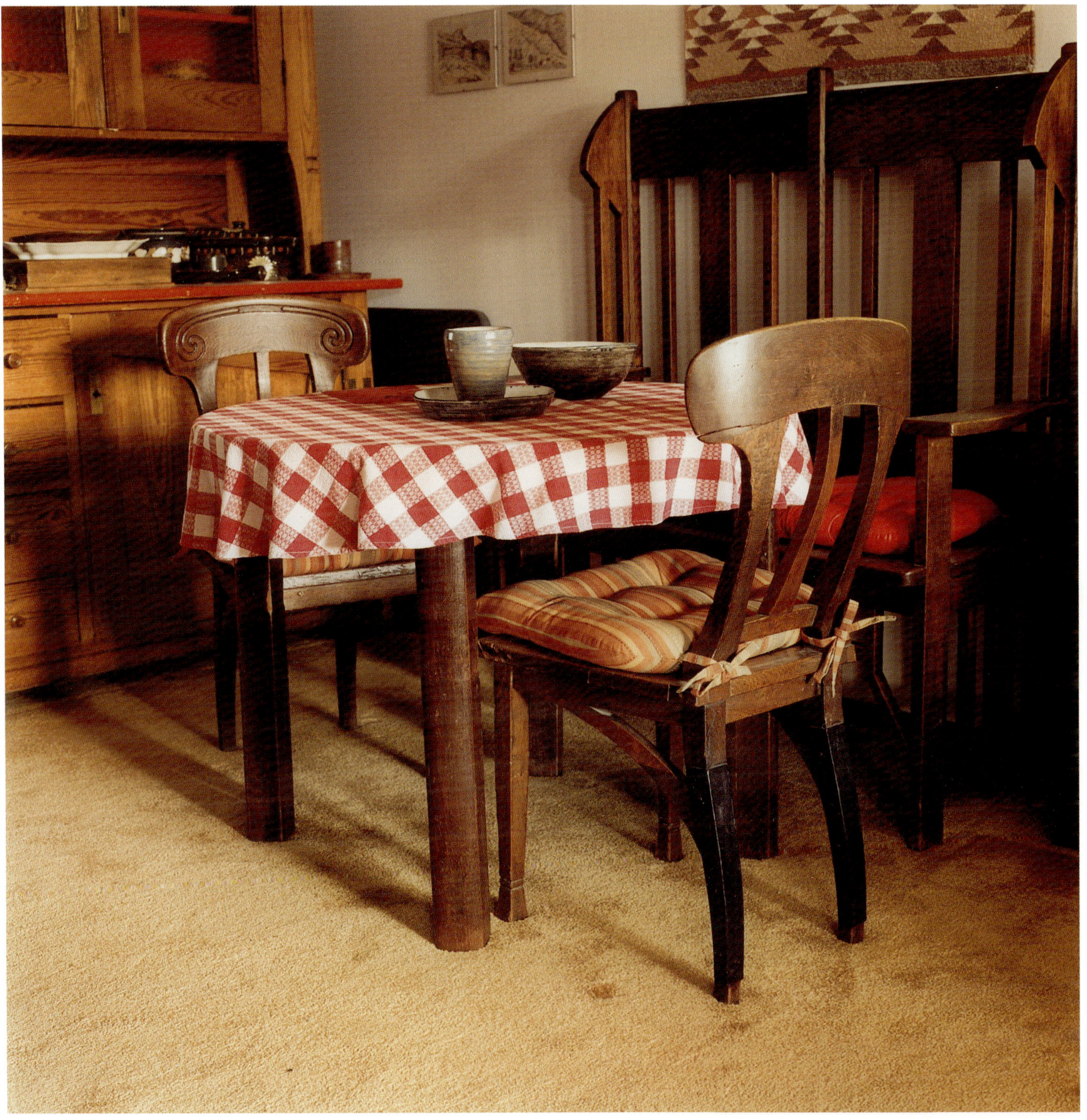

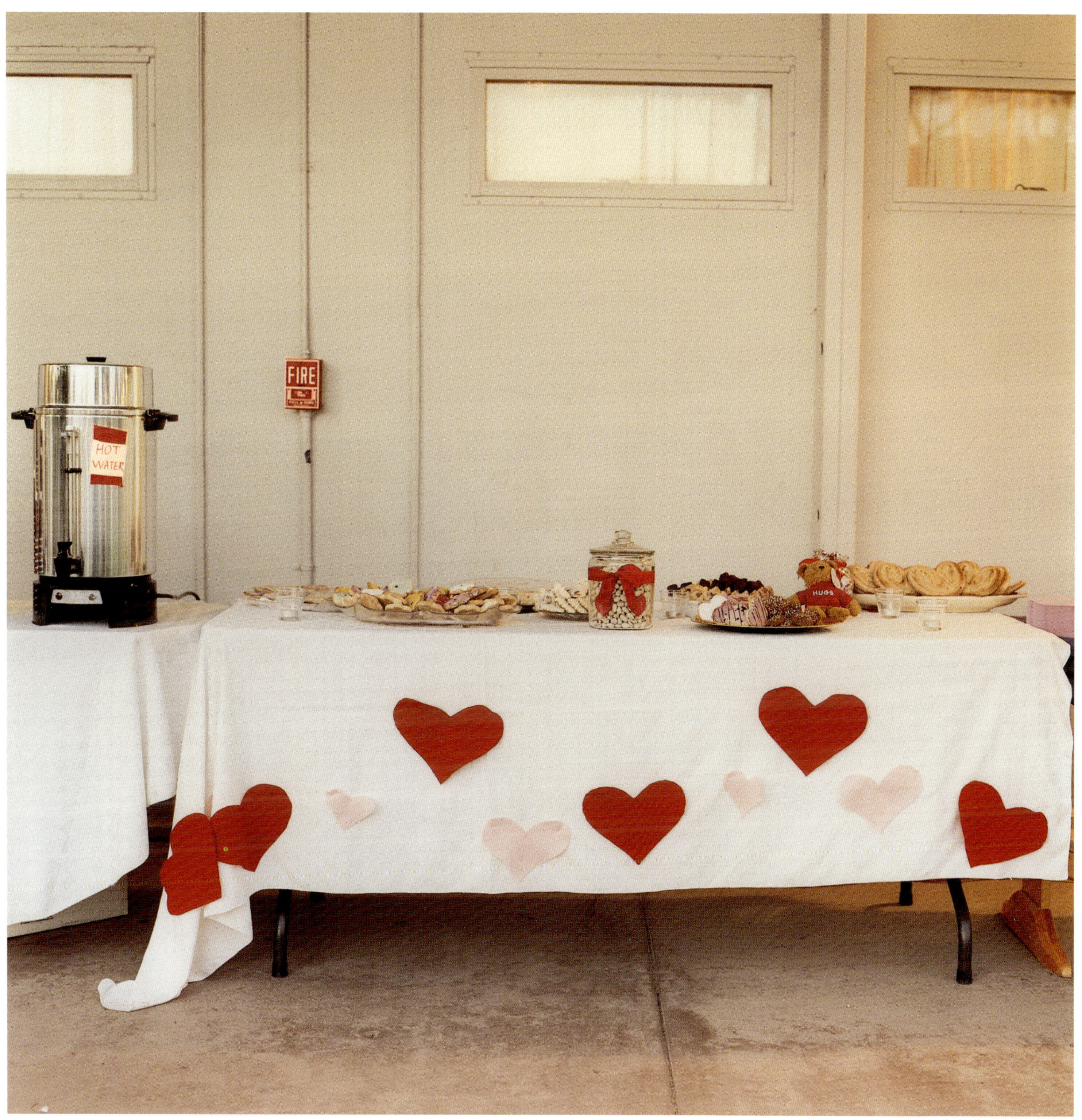
HOT
WATER
FIRE
HUGS

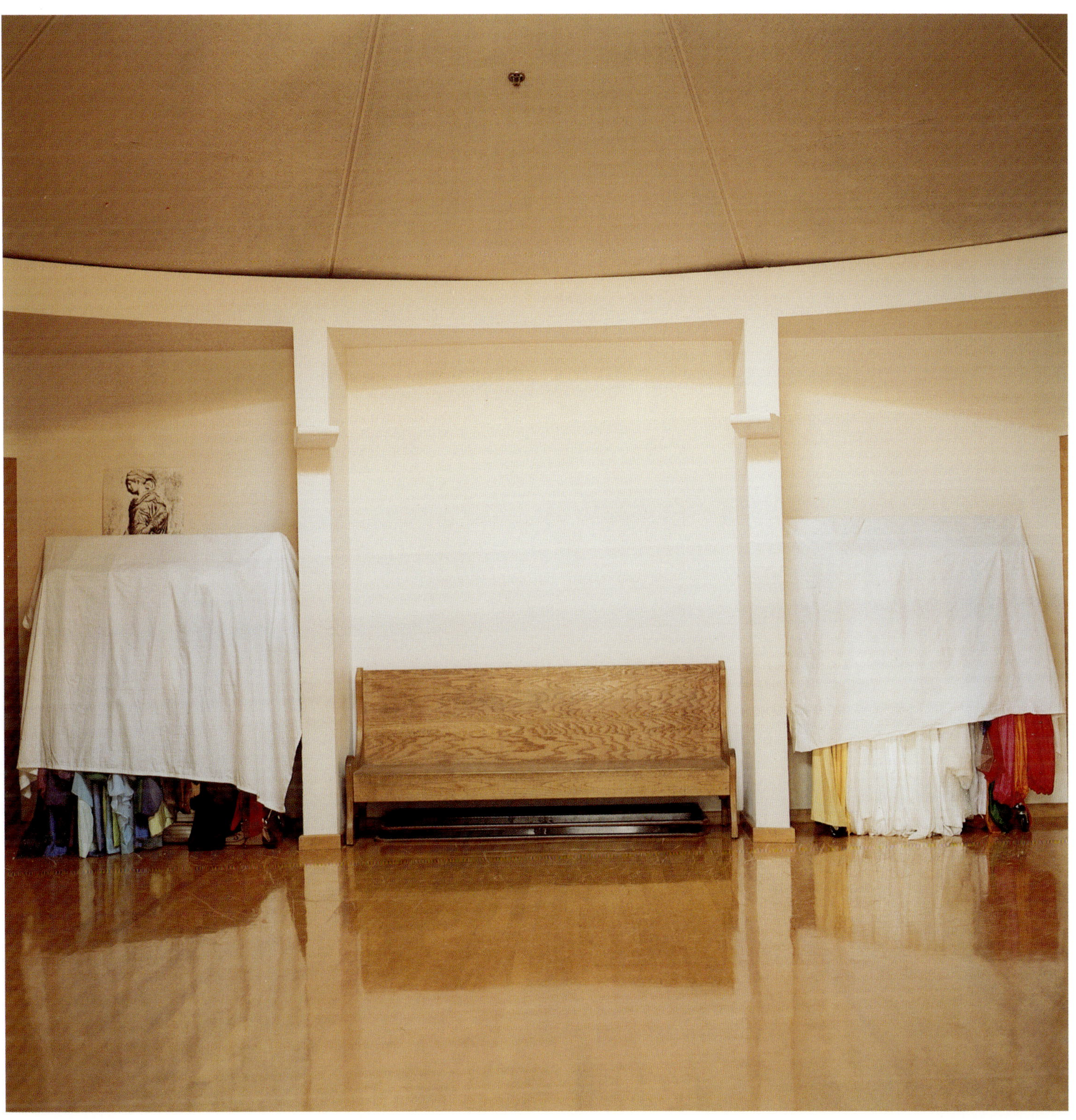

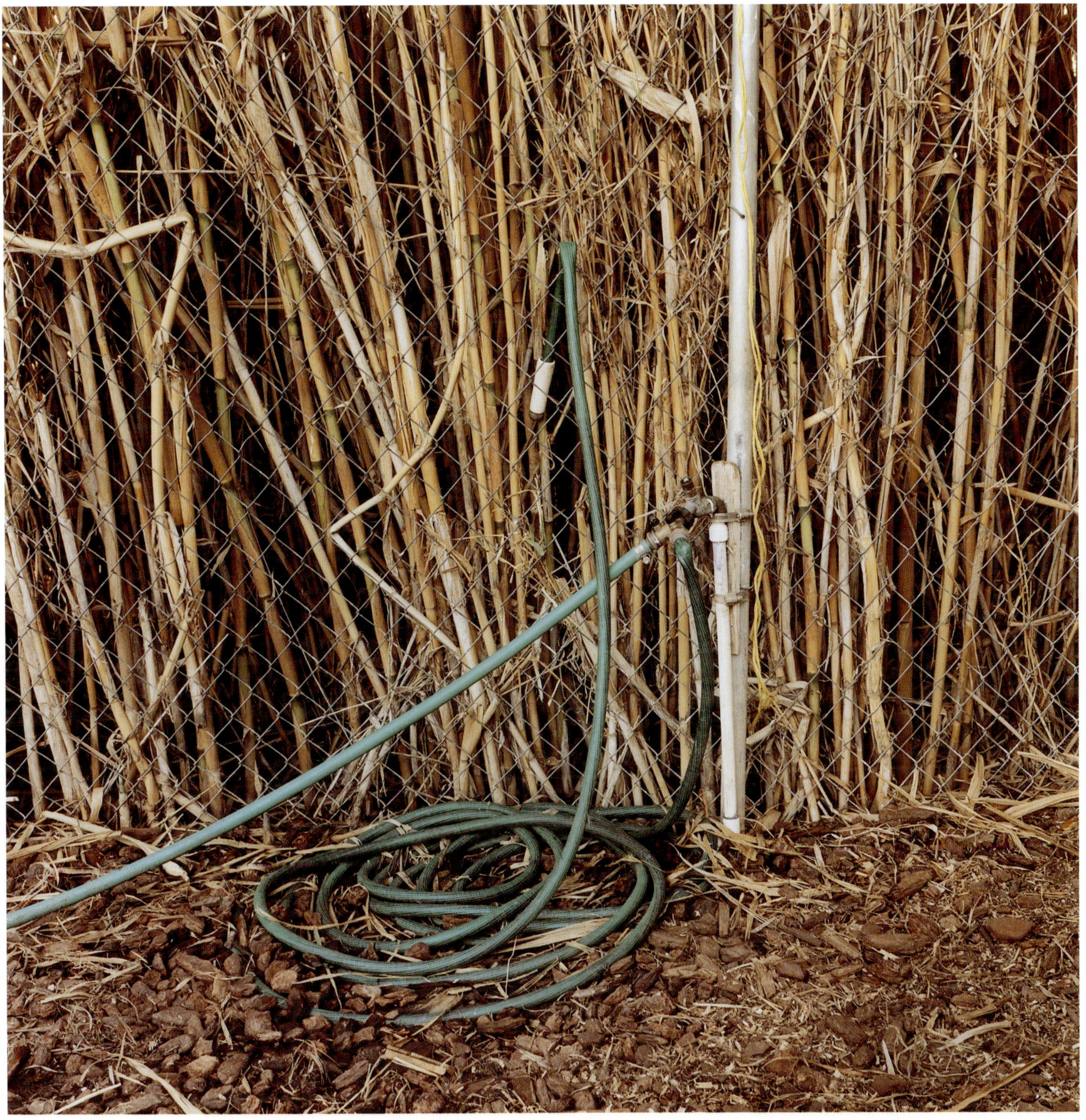

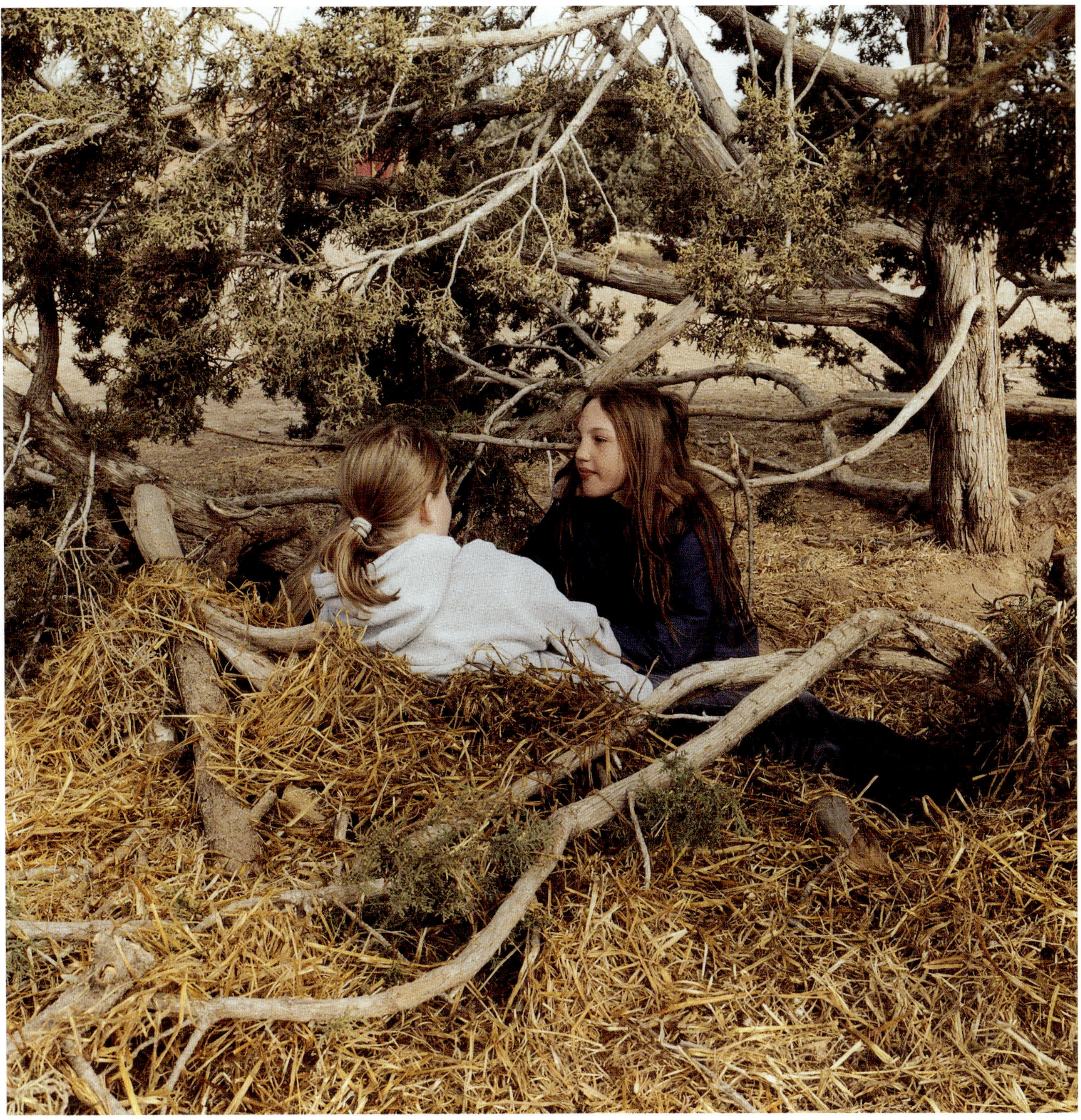

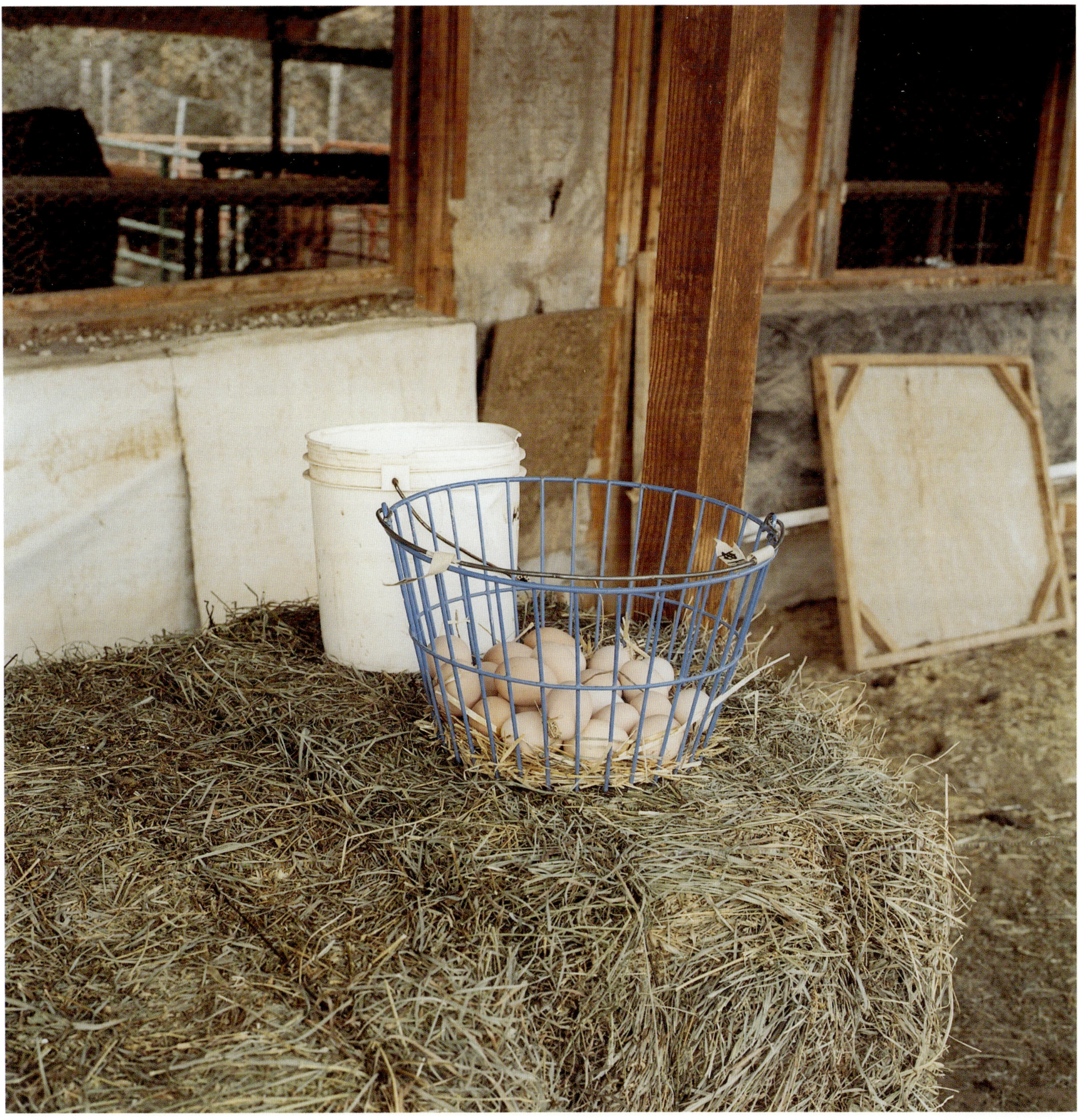

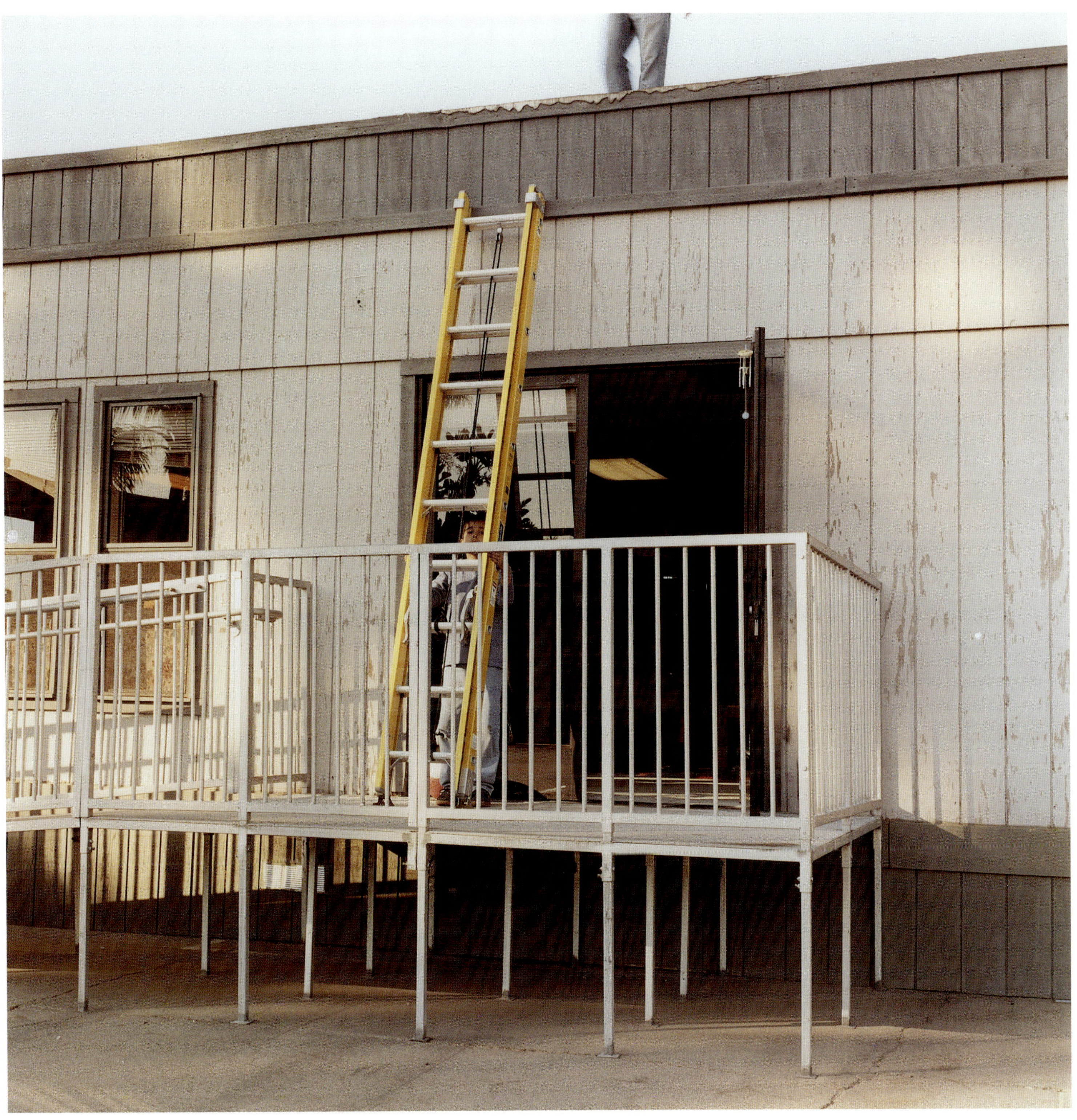

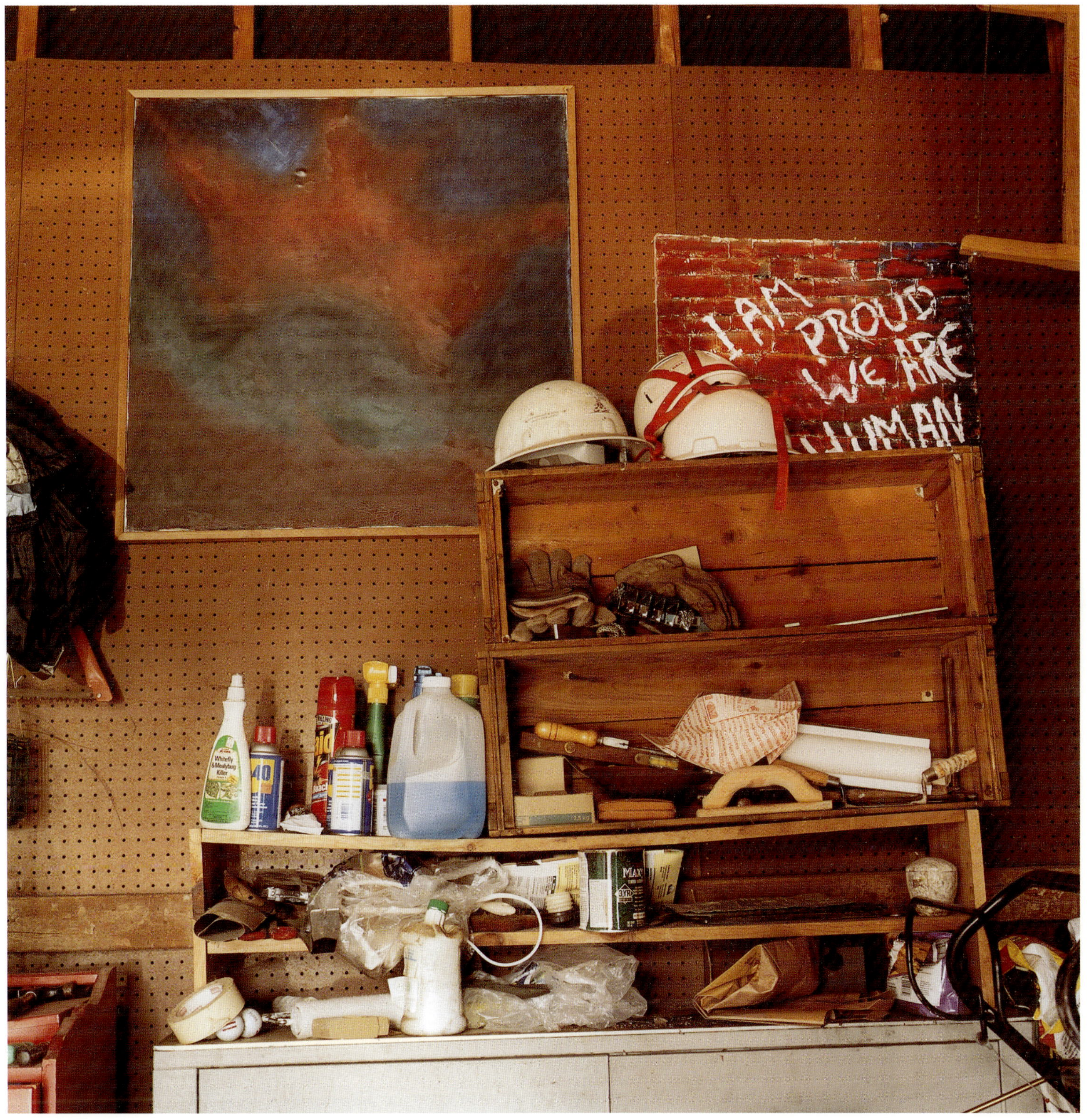

I AM PROUD
WE ARE
HUMAN

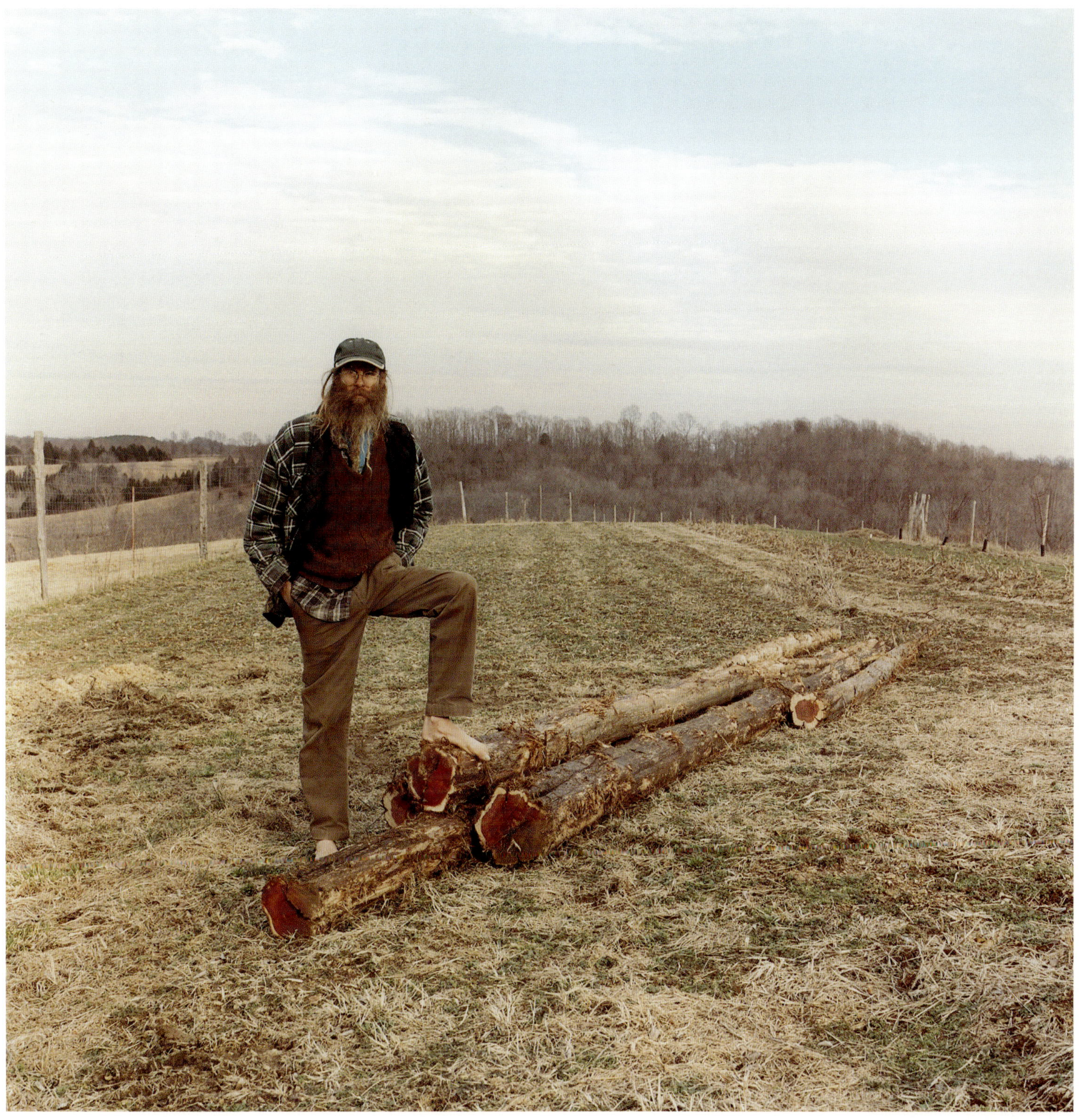

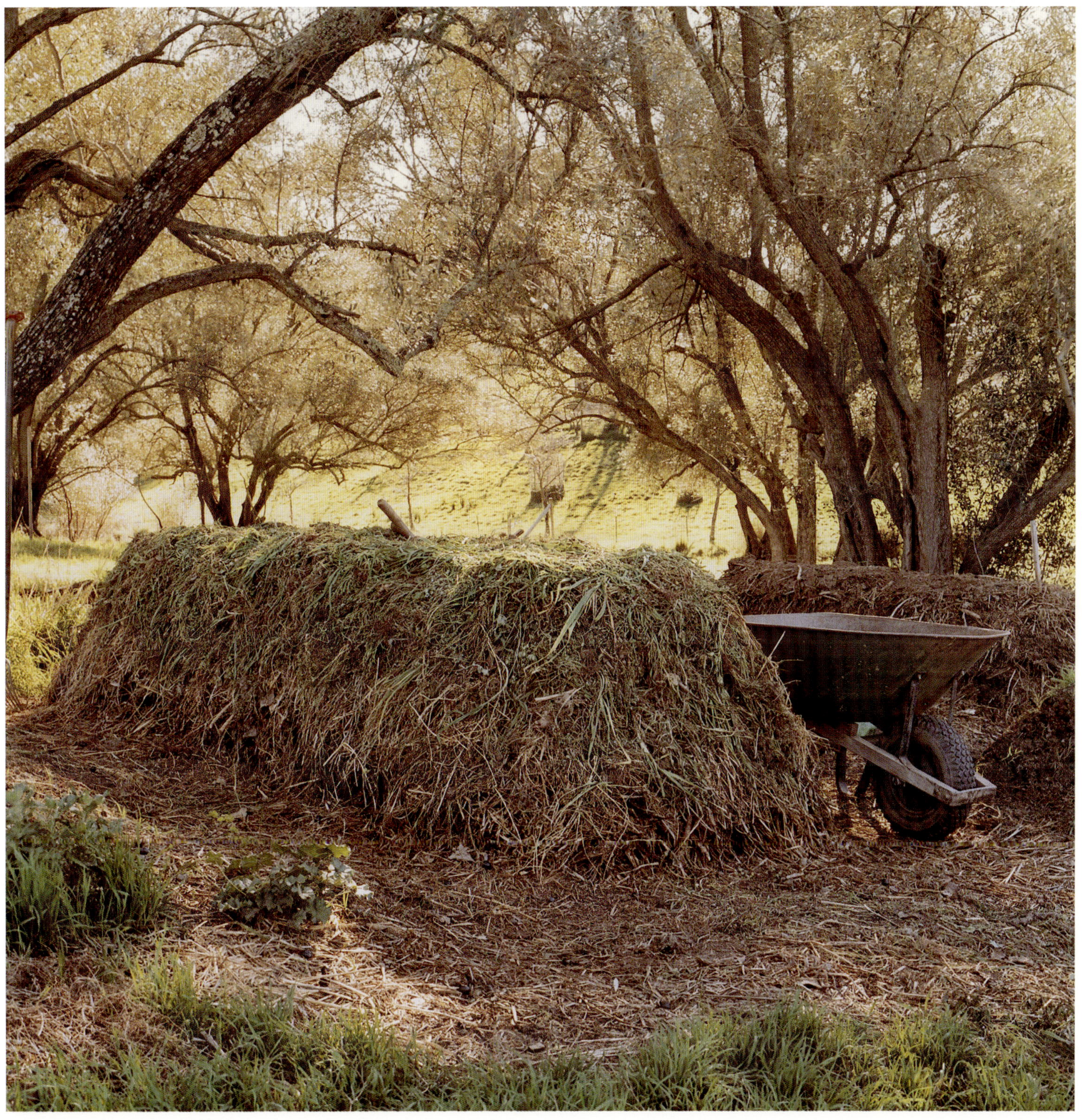

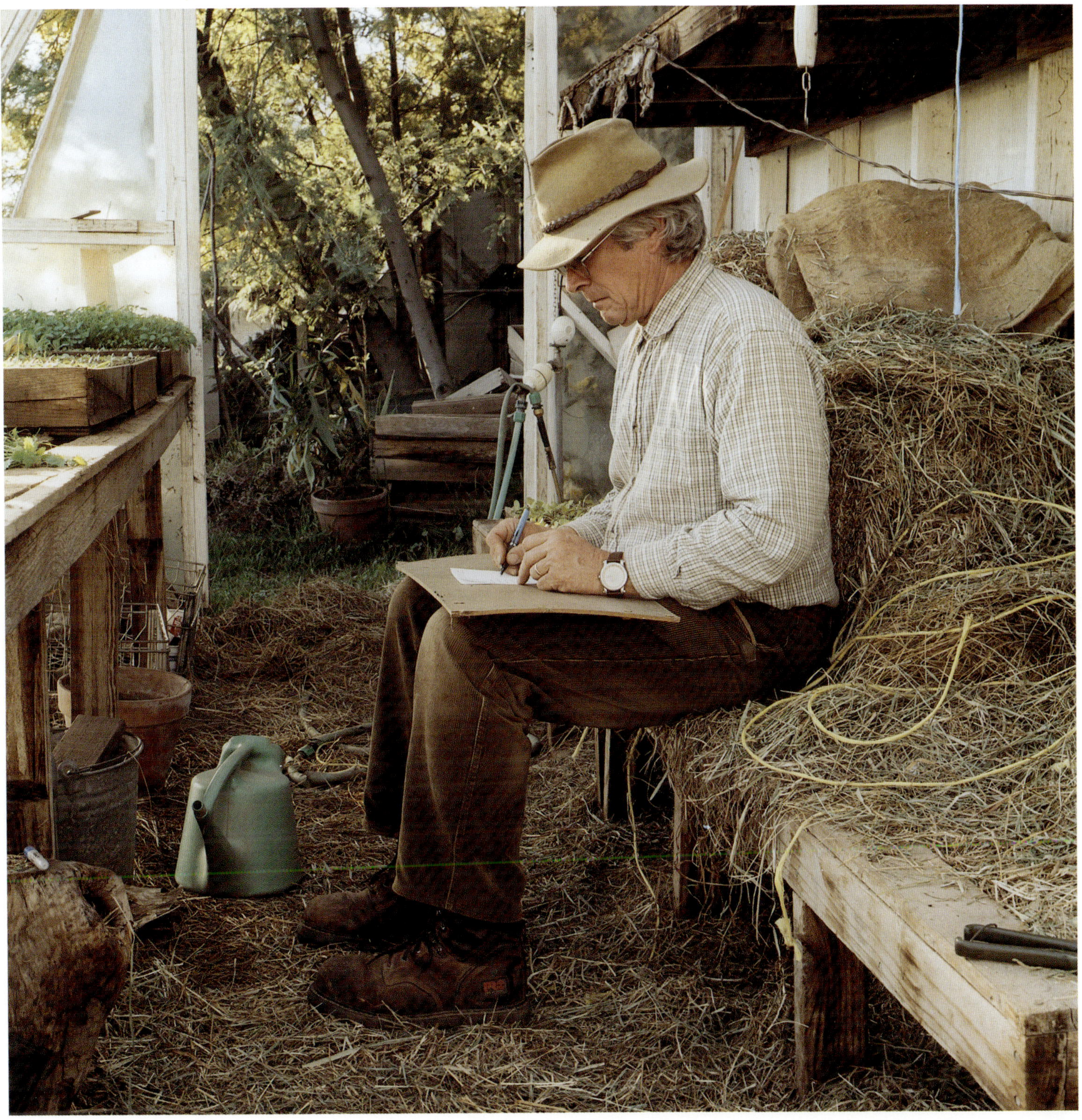

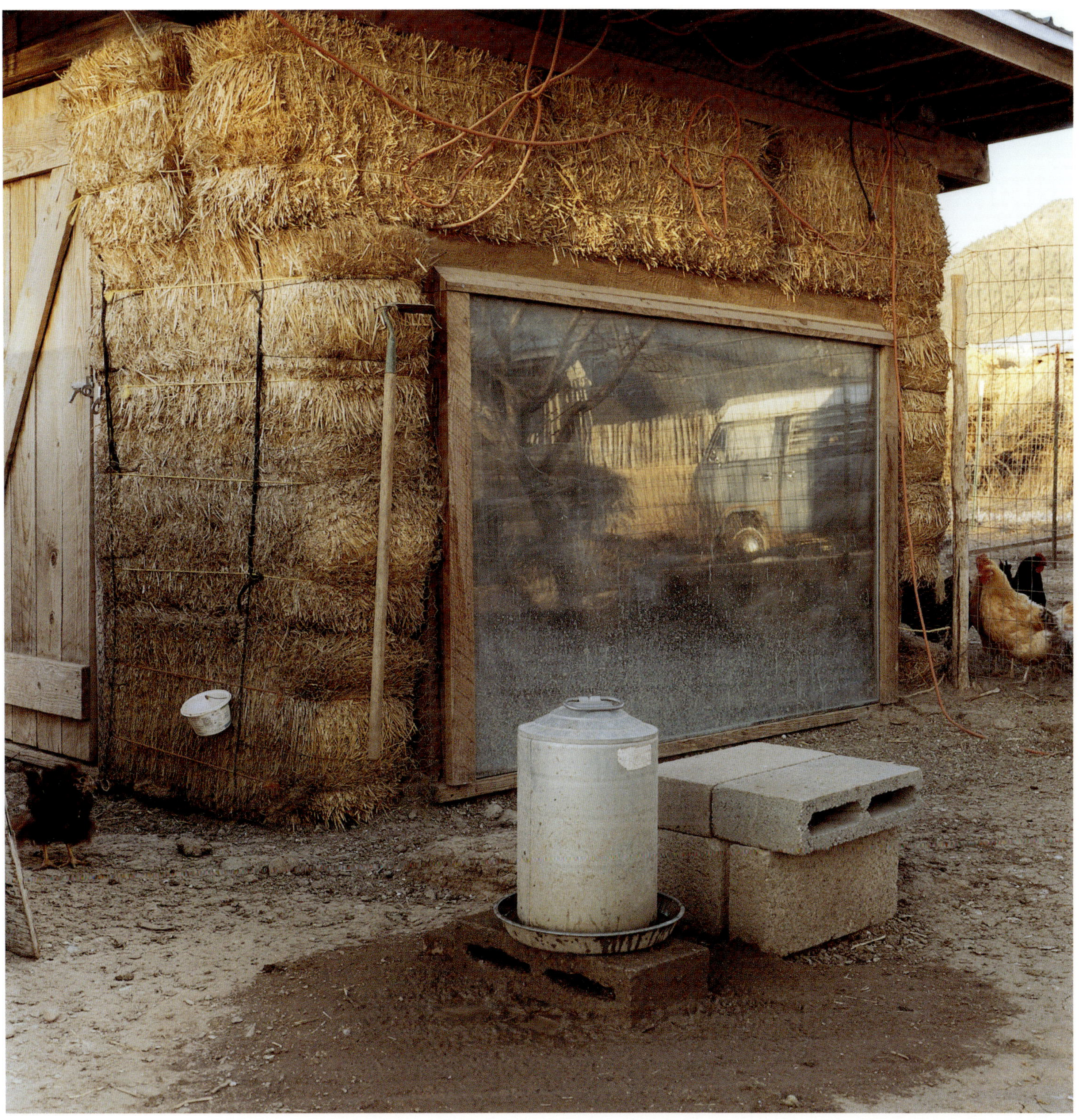

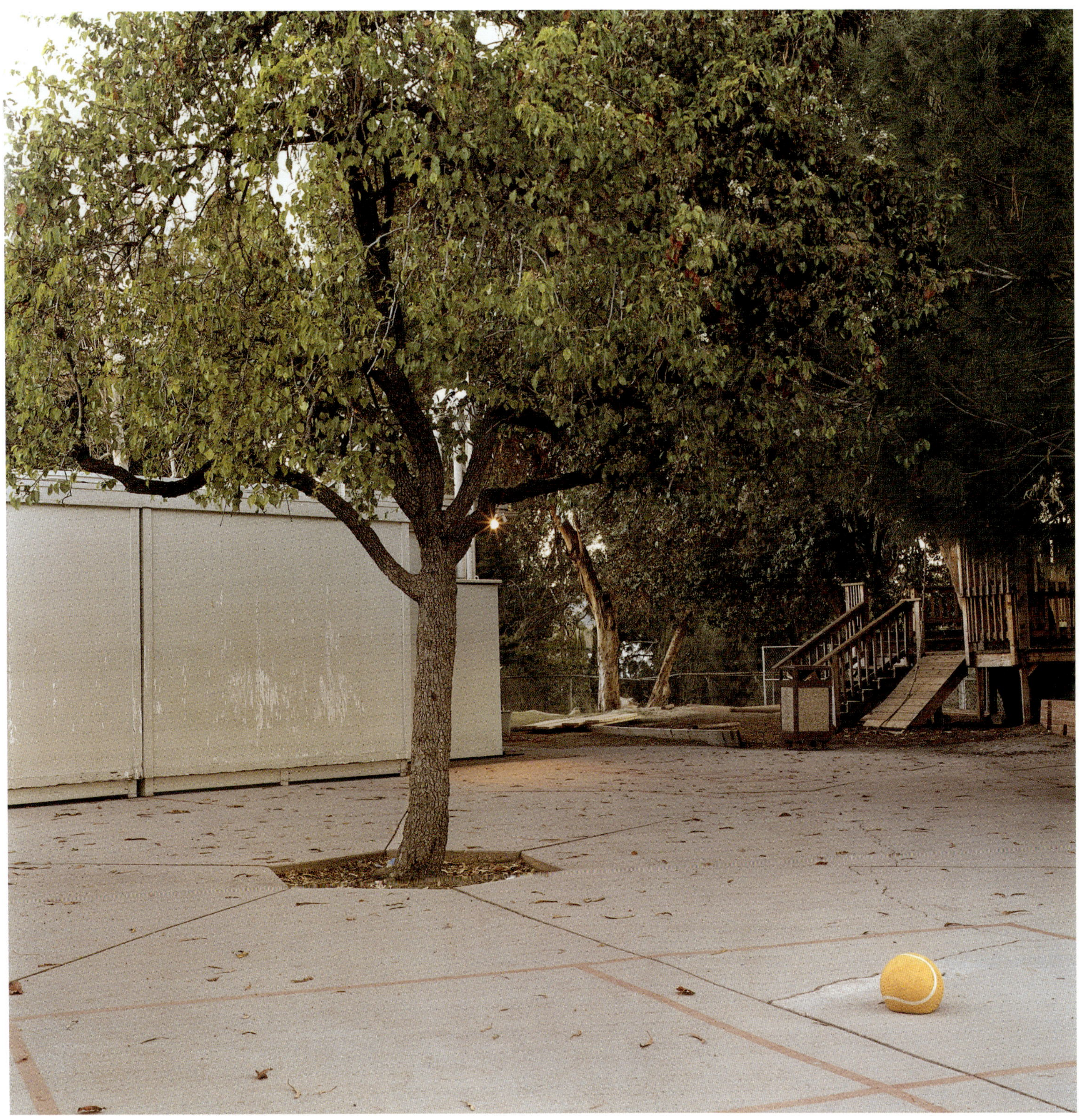

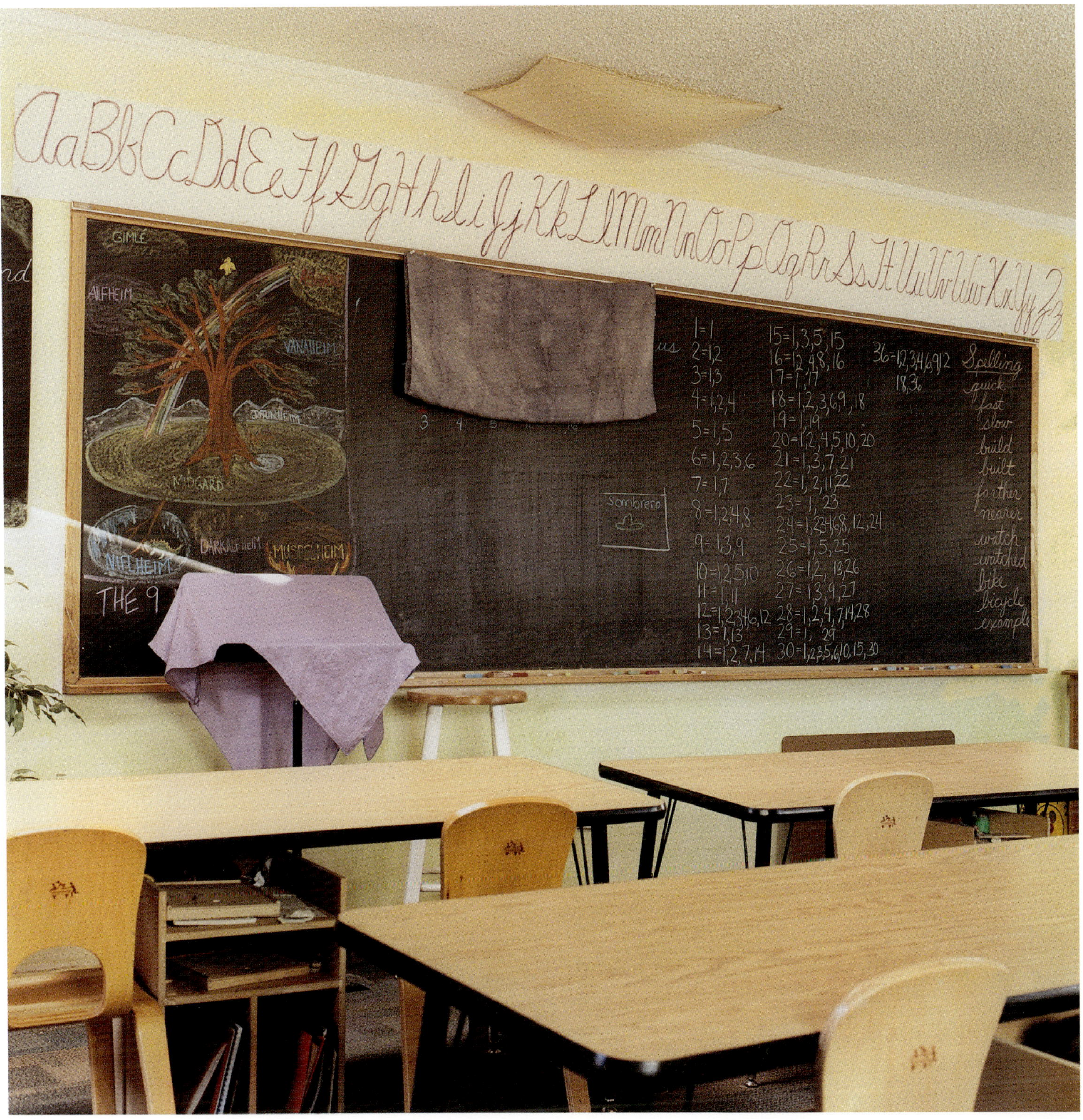

GIMLE
ALFHEIM
VANAHEIM
THRUDHEIM
MIDGARD
NIFLHEIM
DARKALFHEIM
MUSPELHEIM
THE 9
Sombrero
Aa Bb Cc Dd Ee Ff Gg Hh Ii Jj Kk Ll Mm Nn Oo Pp Qq Rr Ss Tt Uu Vv Ww Xx Yy Zz
1=1
2=1,2
3=1,3
4=1,2,4
5=1,5
6=1,2,3,6
7=1,7
8=1,2,4,8
9=1,3,9
10=1,2,5,10
11=1,11
12=1,2,3,4,6,12
13=1,13
14=1,2,7,14
15=1,3,5,15
16=1,2,4,8,16
17=1,17
18=1,2,3,6,9,18
19=1,19
20=1,2,4,5,10,20
21=1,3,7,21
22=1,2,11,22
23=1,23
24=1,2,3,4,6,8,12,24
25=1,5,25
26=1,2,13,26
27=1,3,9,27
28=1,2,4,7,14,28
29=1,29
30=1,2,3,5,6,10,15,30
36=1,2,3,4,6,9,12,18,36
Spelling
quick
fast
slow
build
built
farther
nearer
watch
watched
bike
bicycle
example

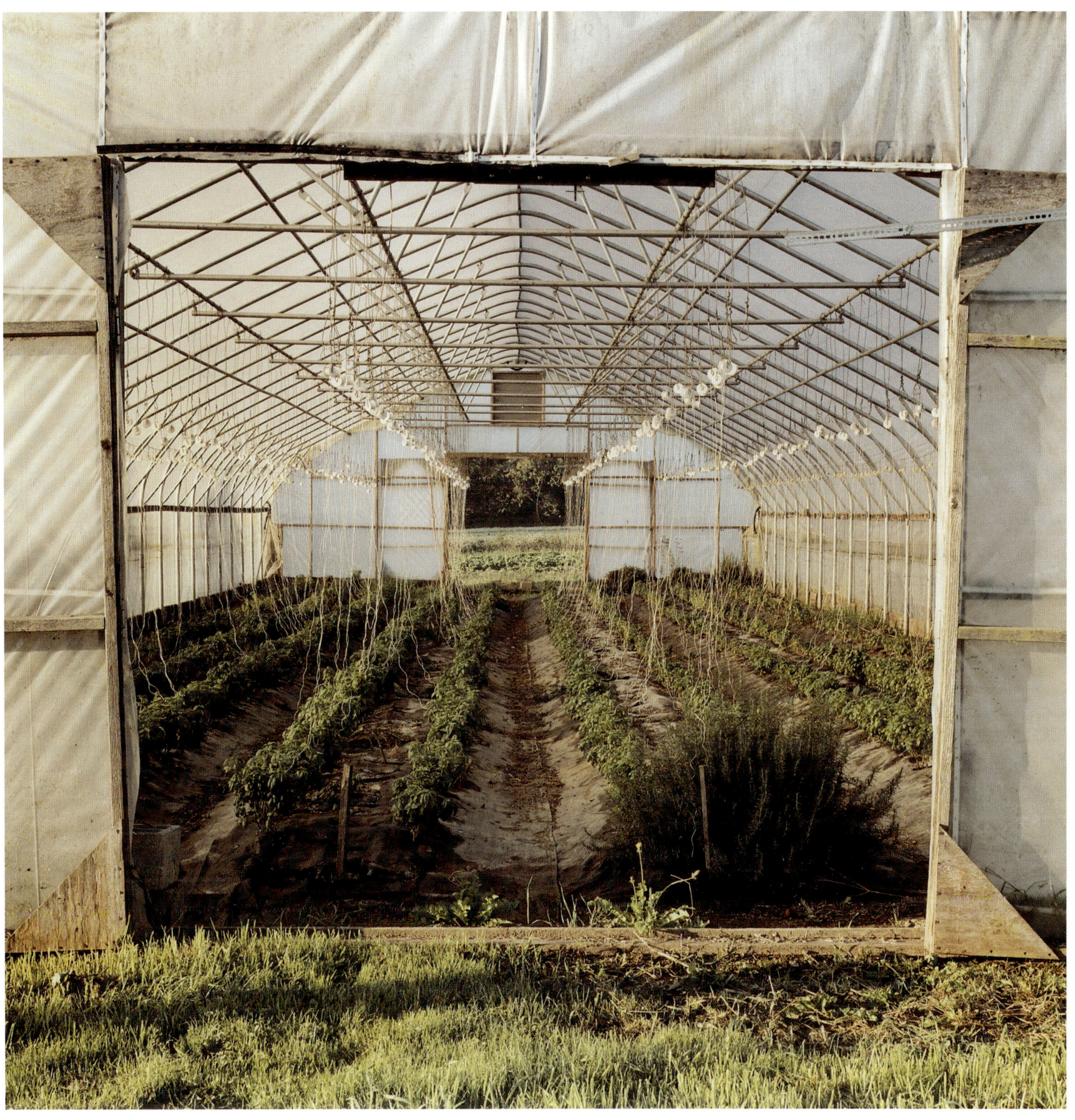

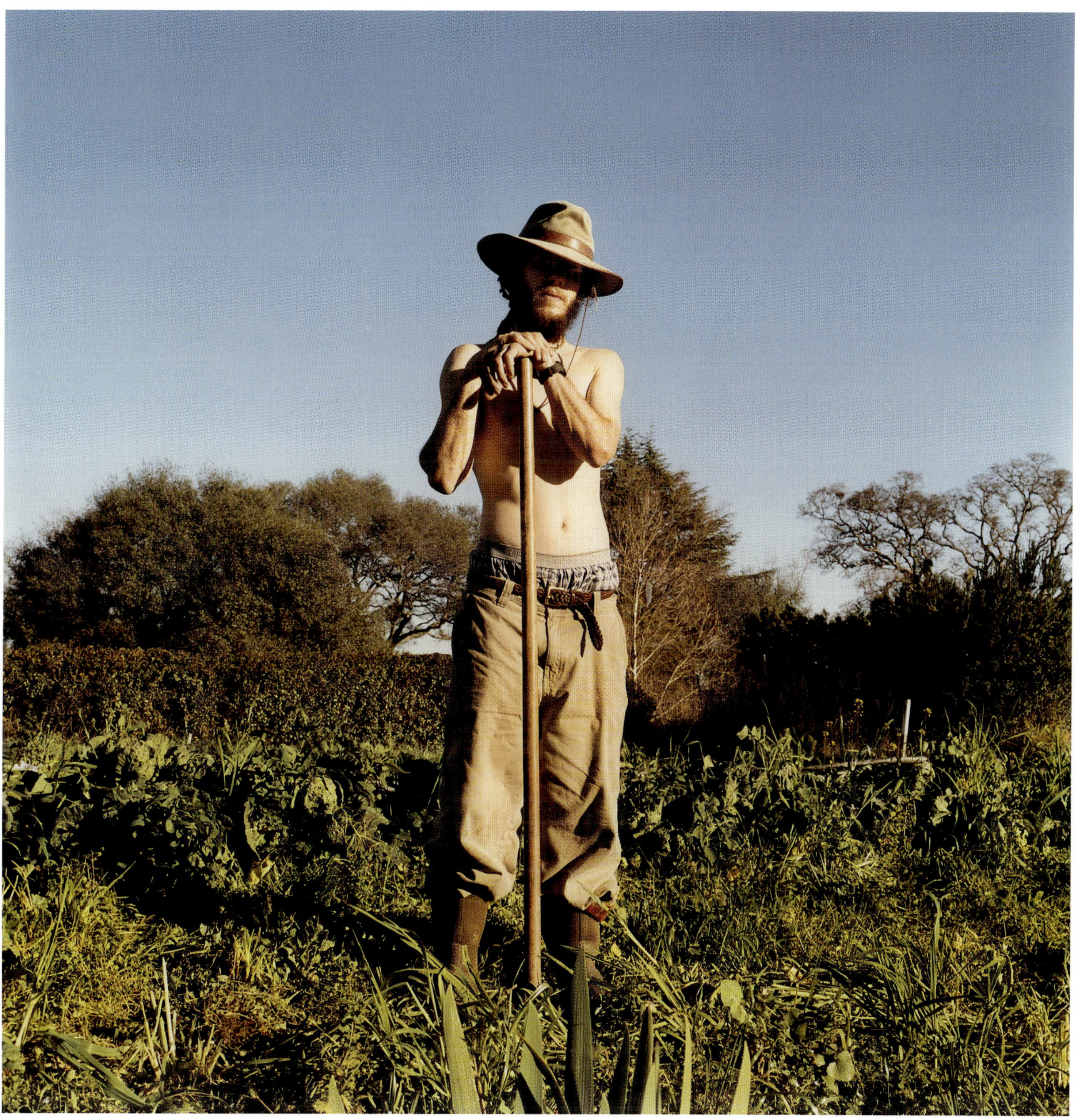

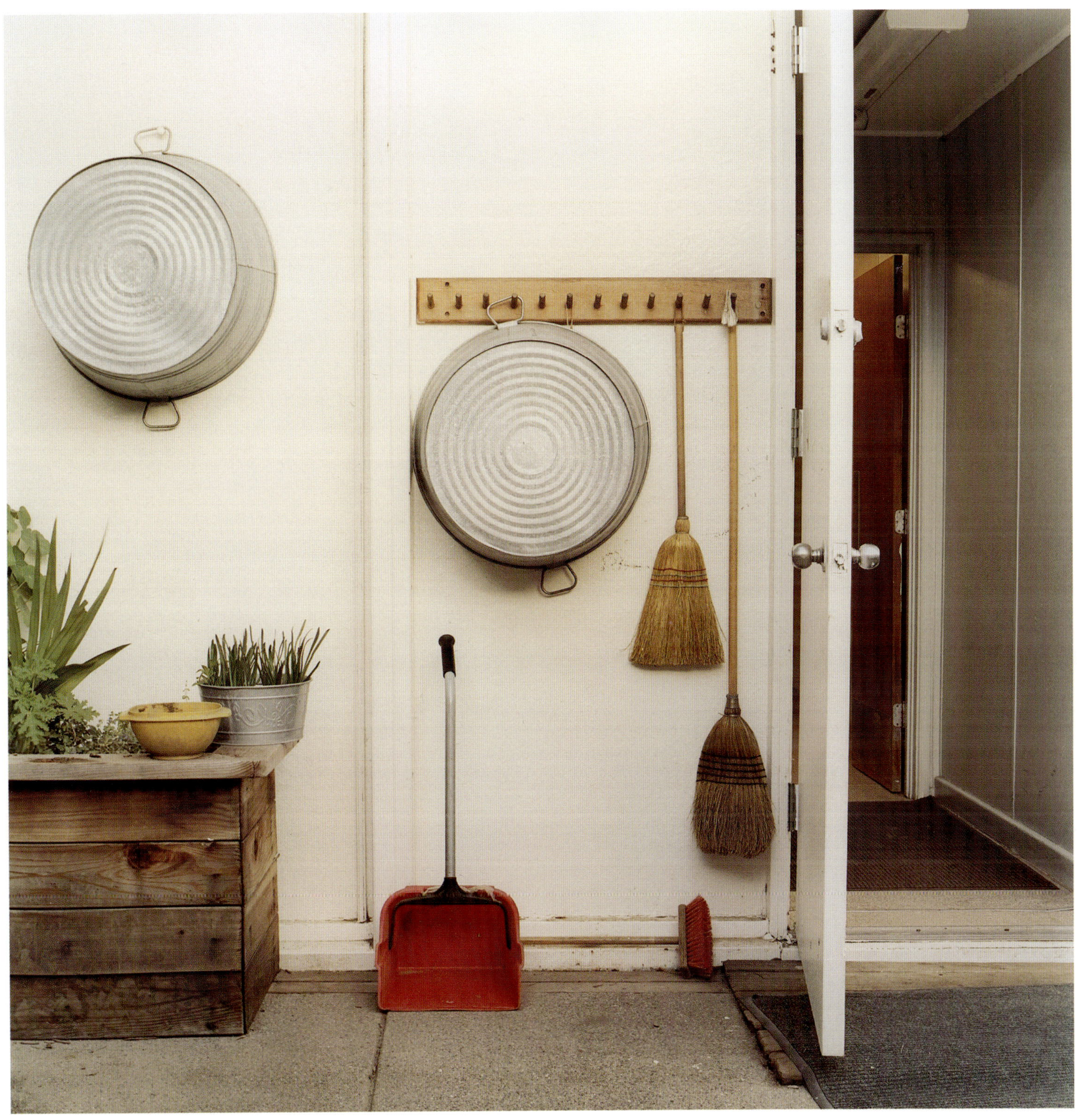

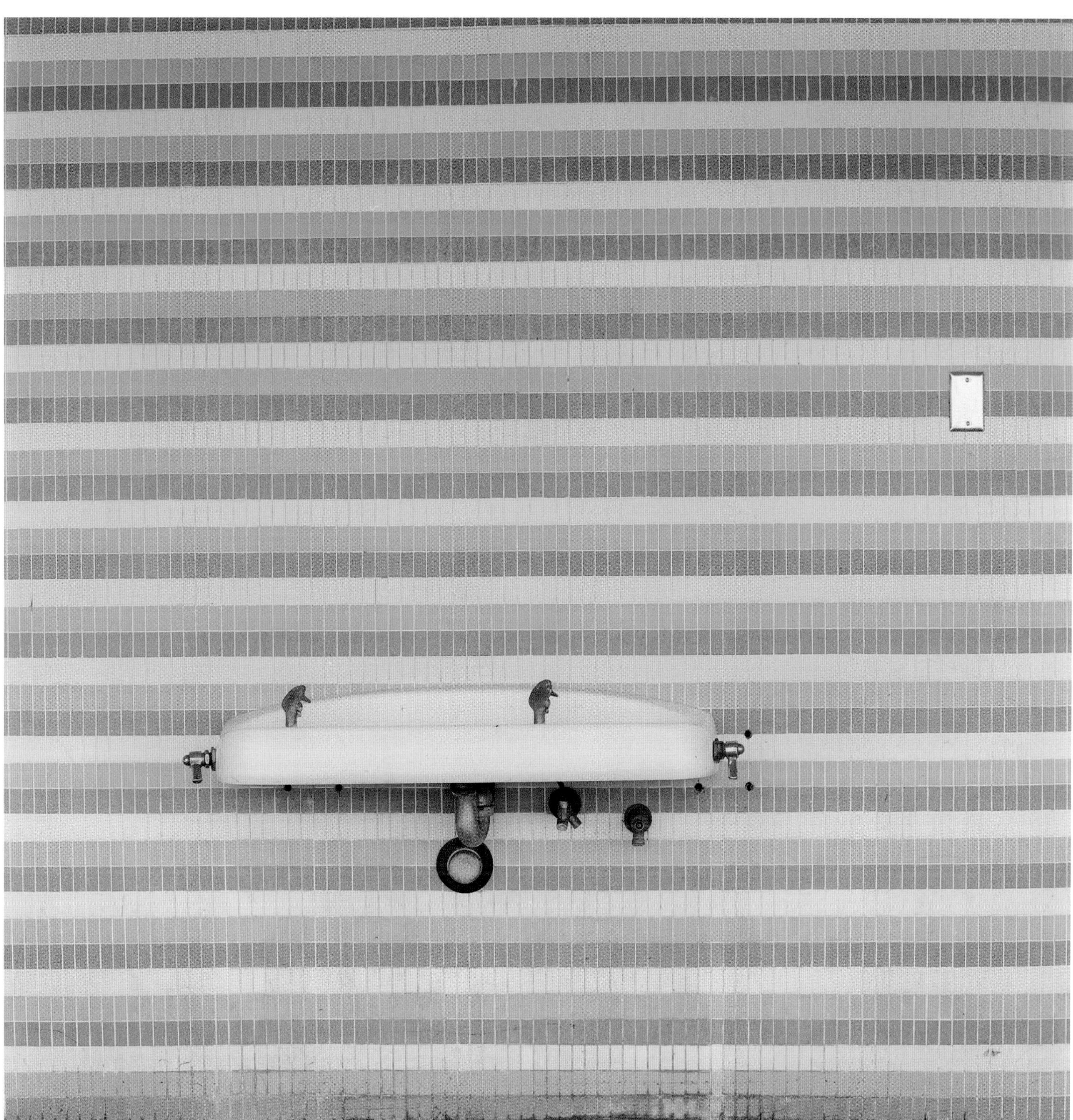

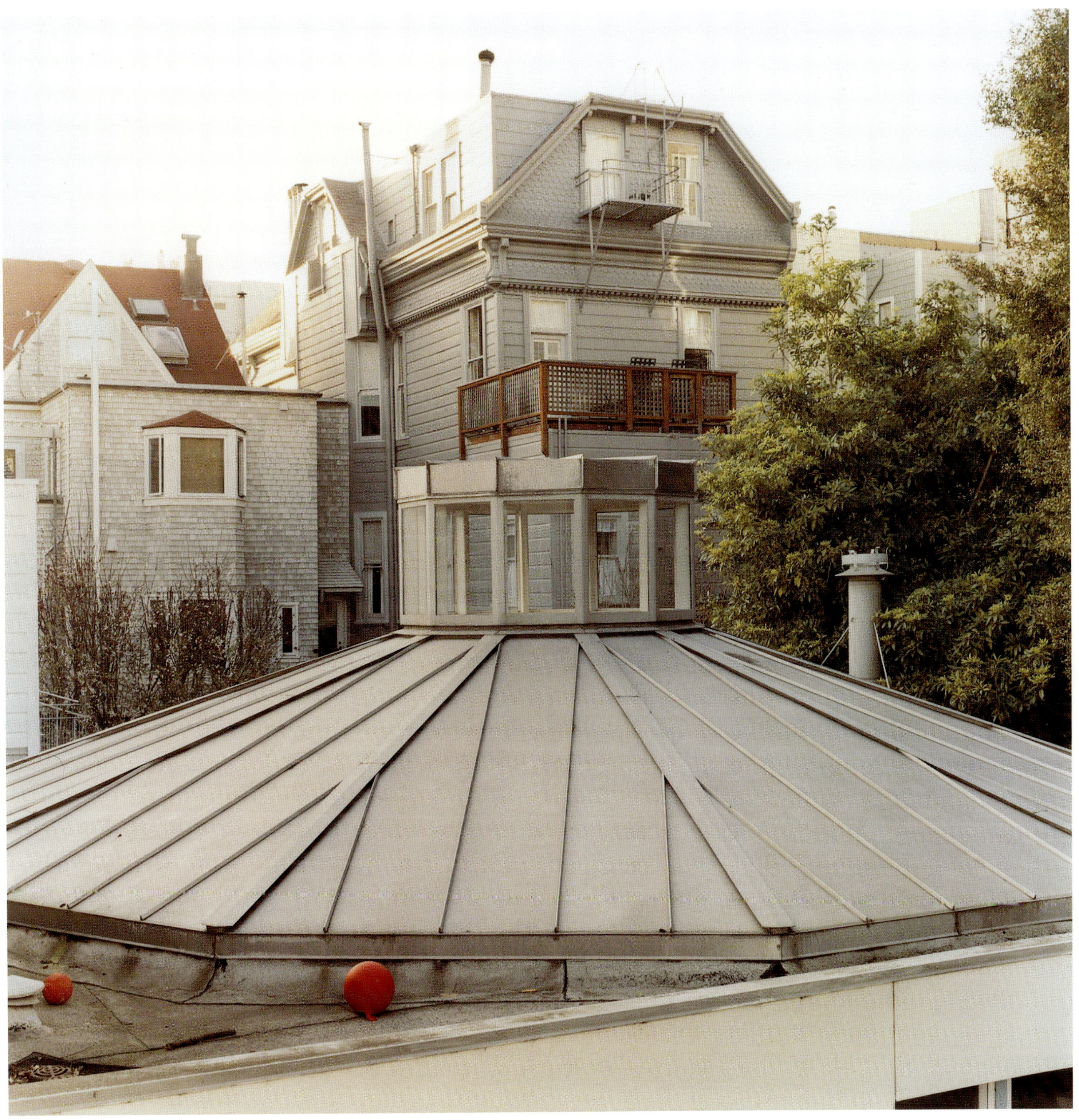

We help each other
and use kind words.
Hands and bodies to
ourselves in line and
in the classroom.
Stand quietly and
face forward.
Listen well and
raise your hand.
Everyone does the
best they can.
We will buy 2
trios of rabbits
$60.00 each = $120.00
Each child will
earn and bring
$6.10.

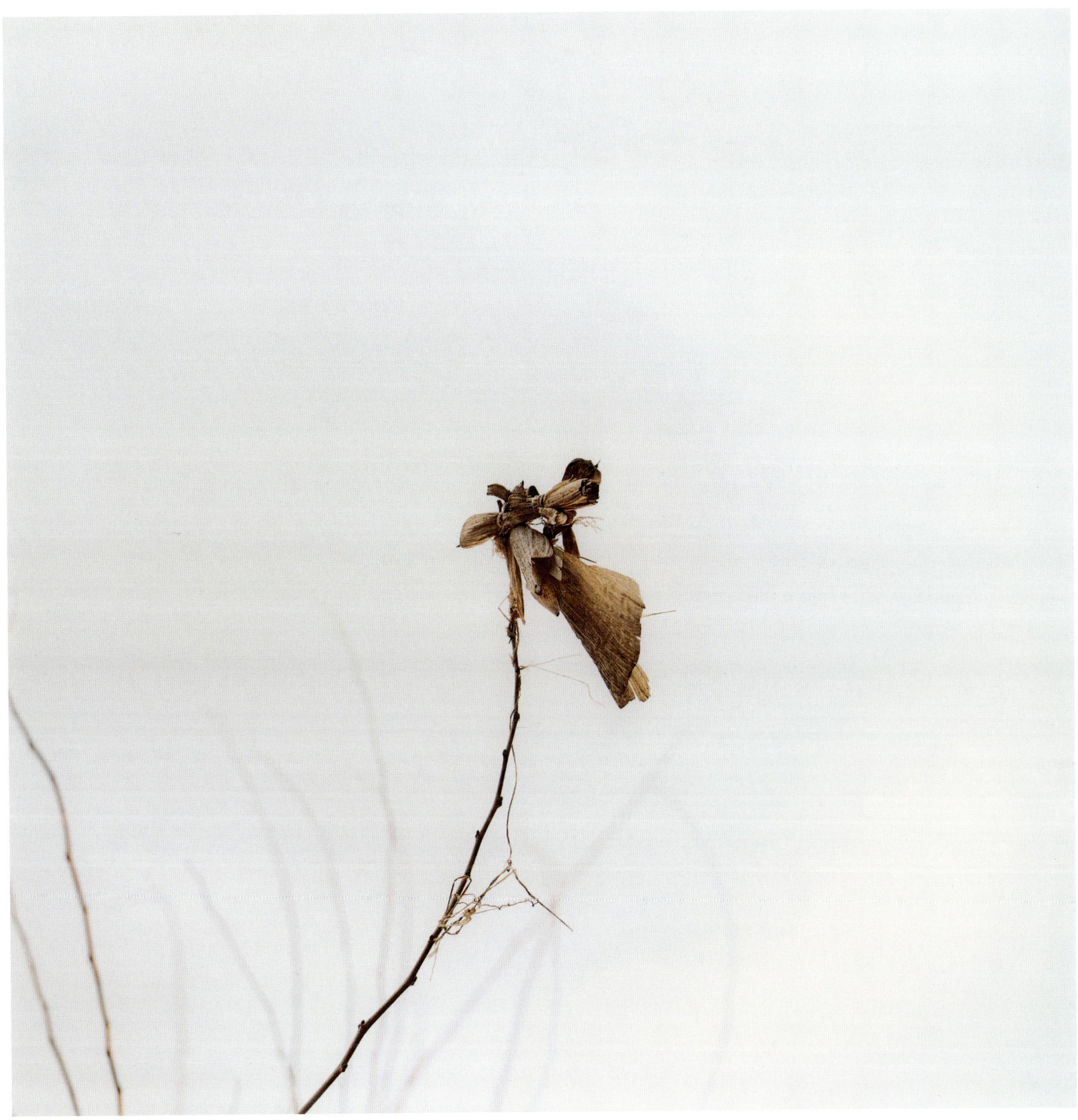

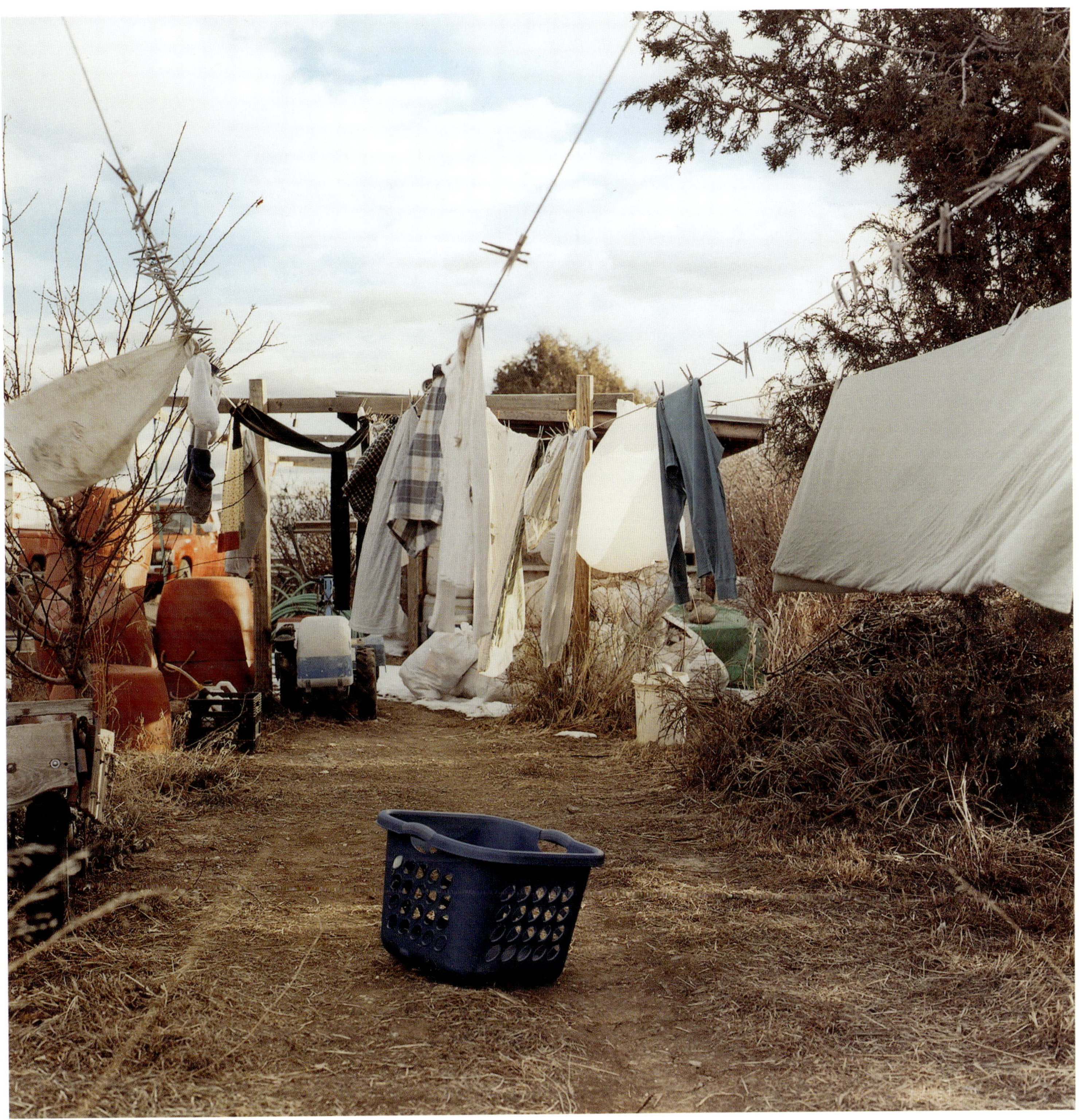

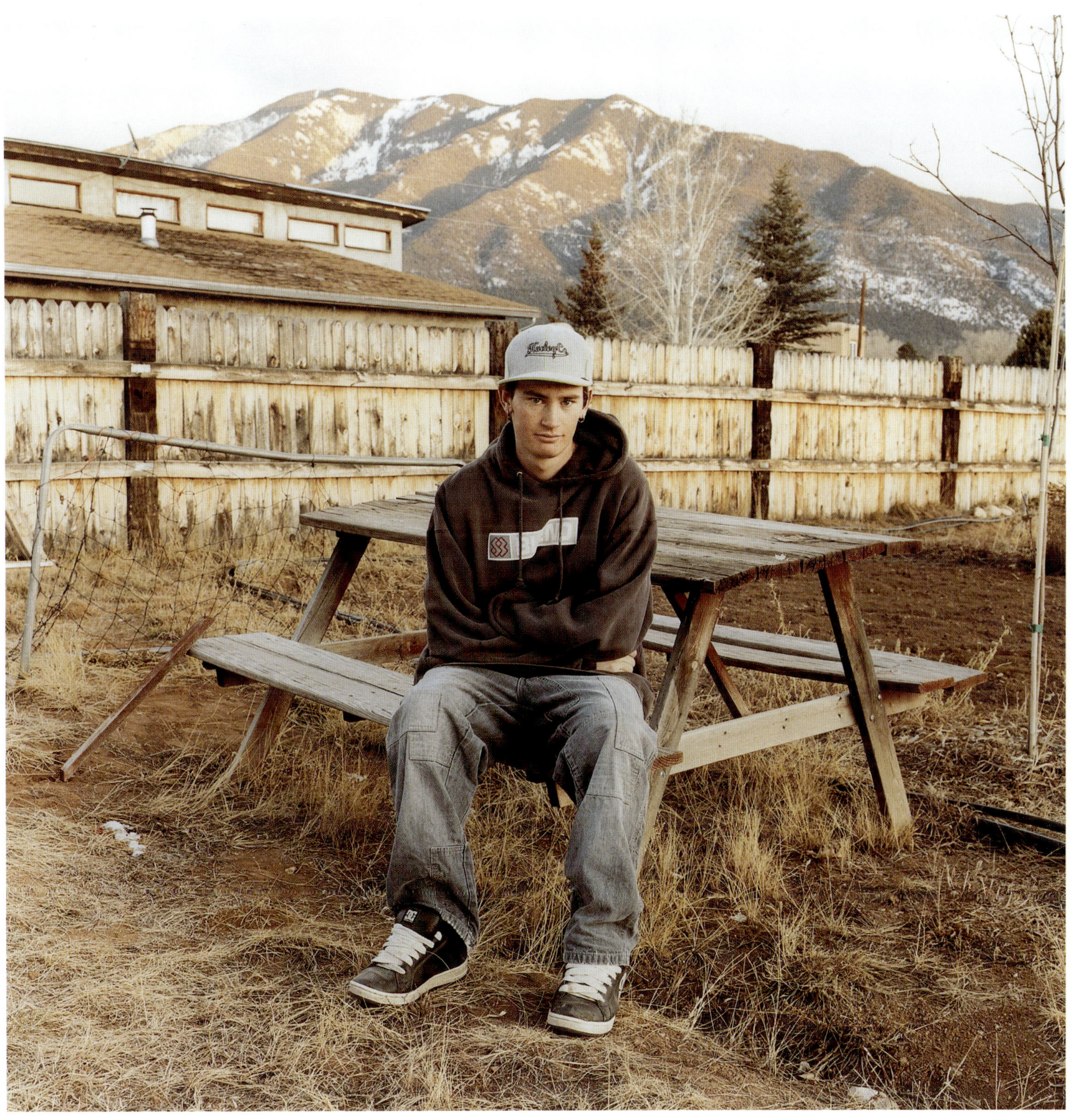

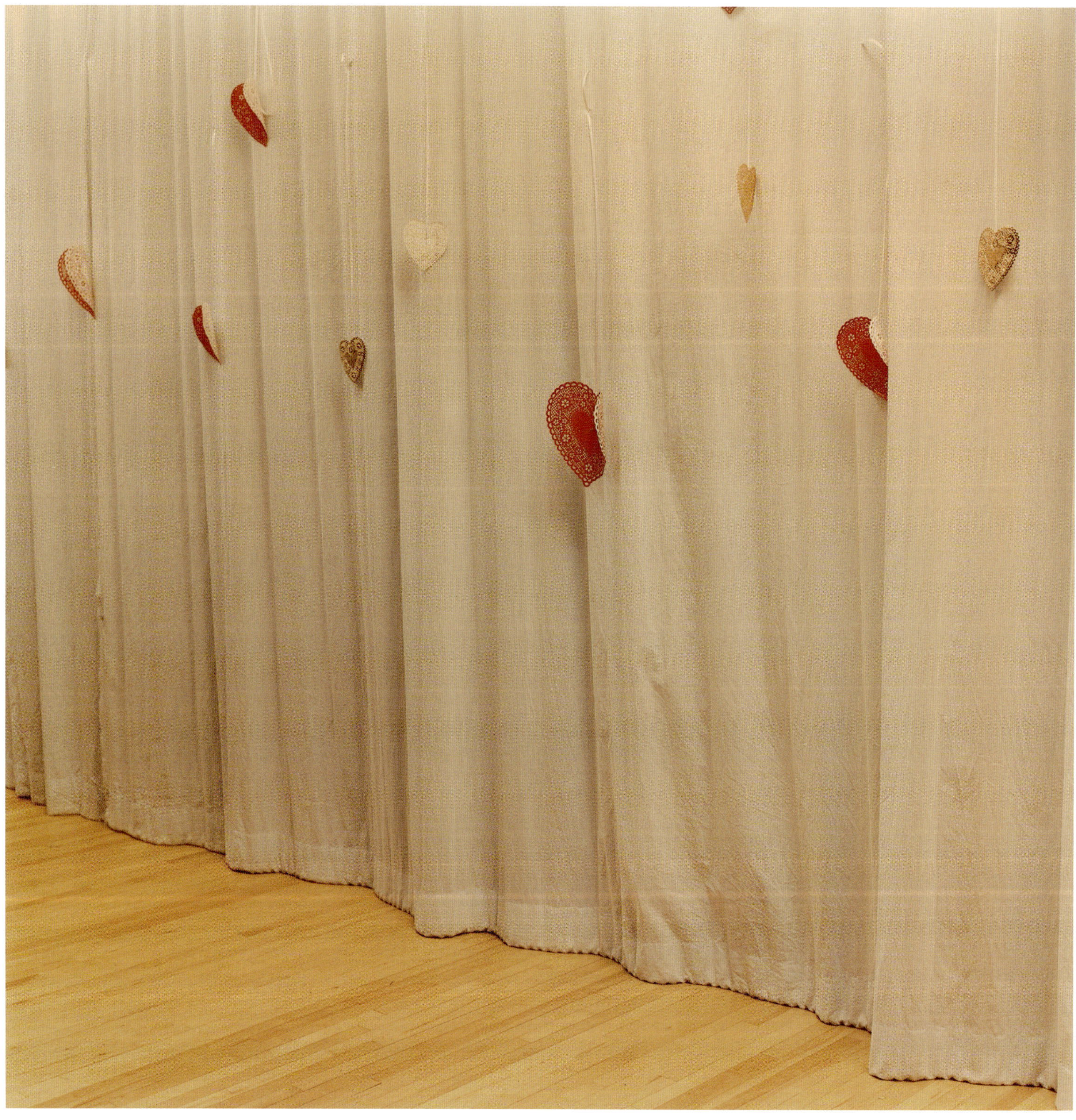

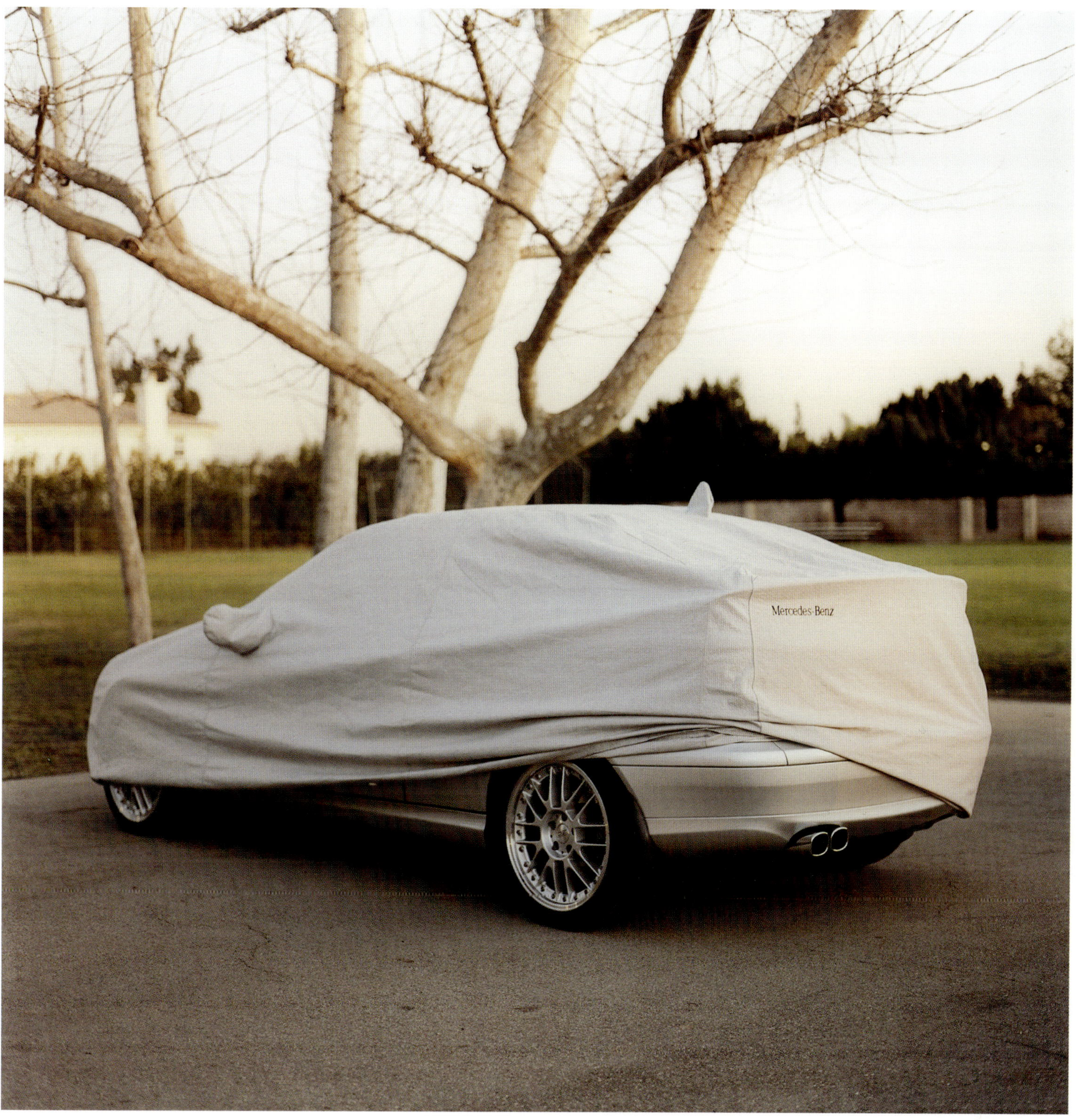

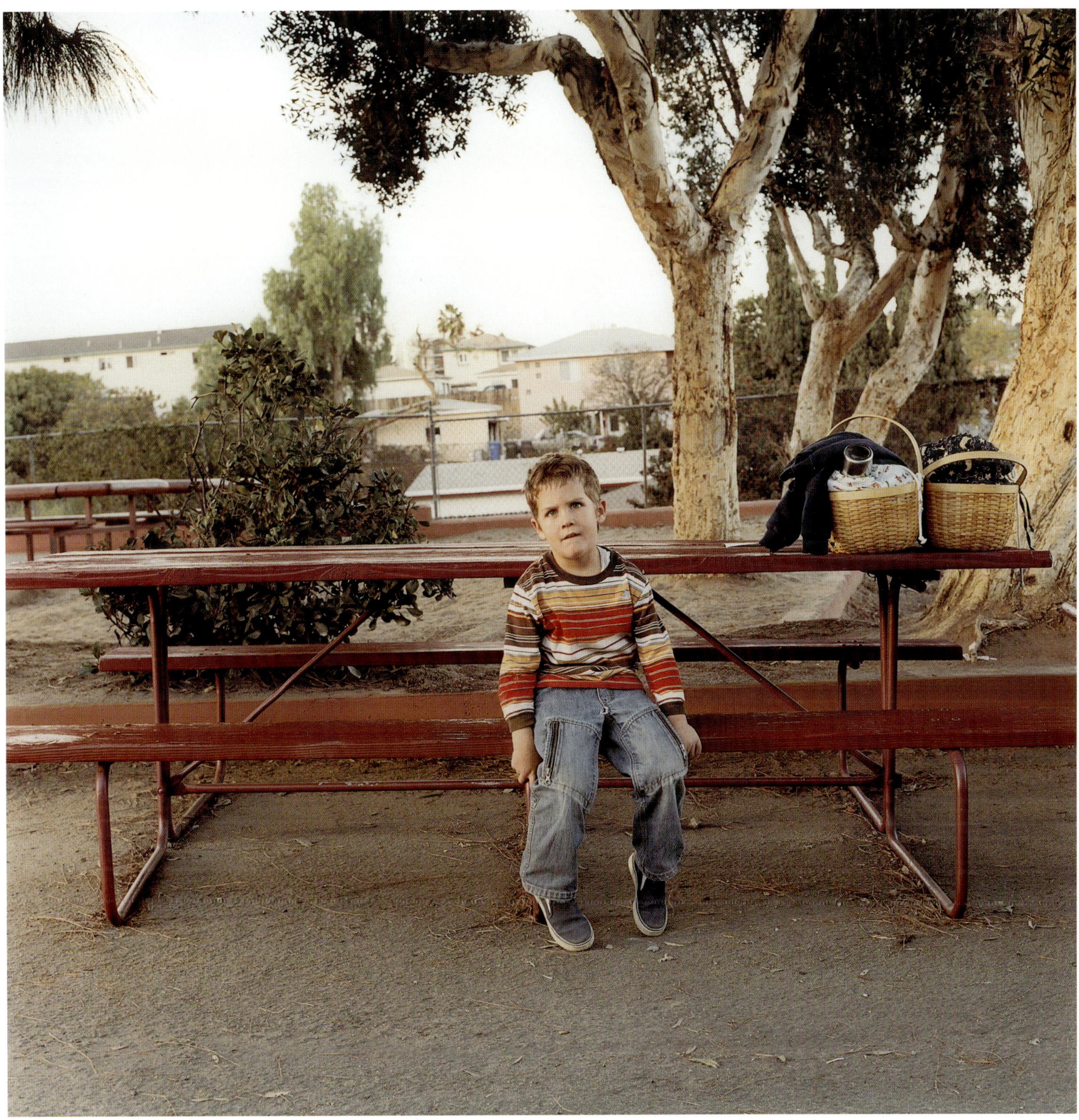

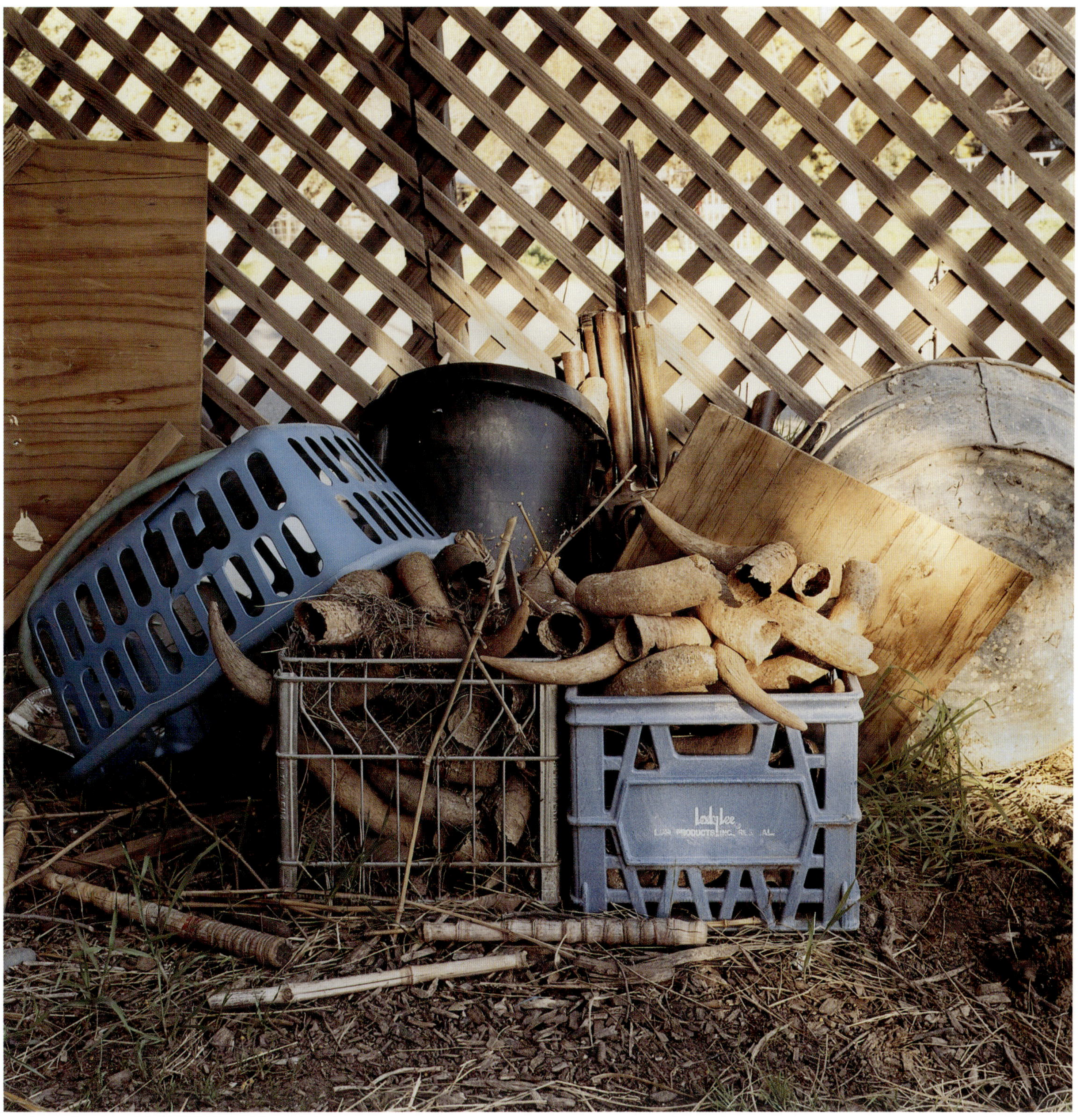

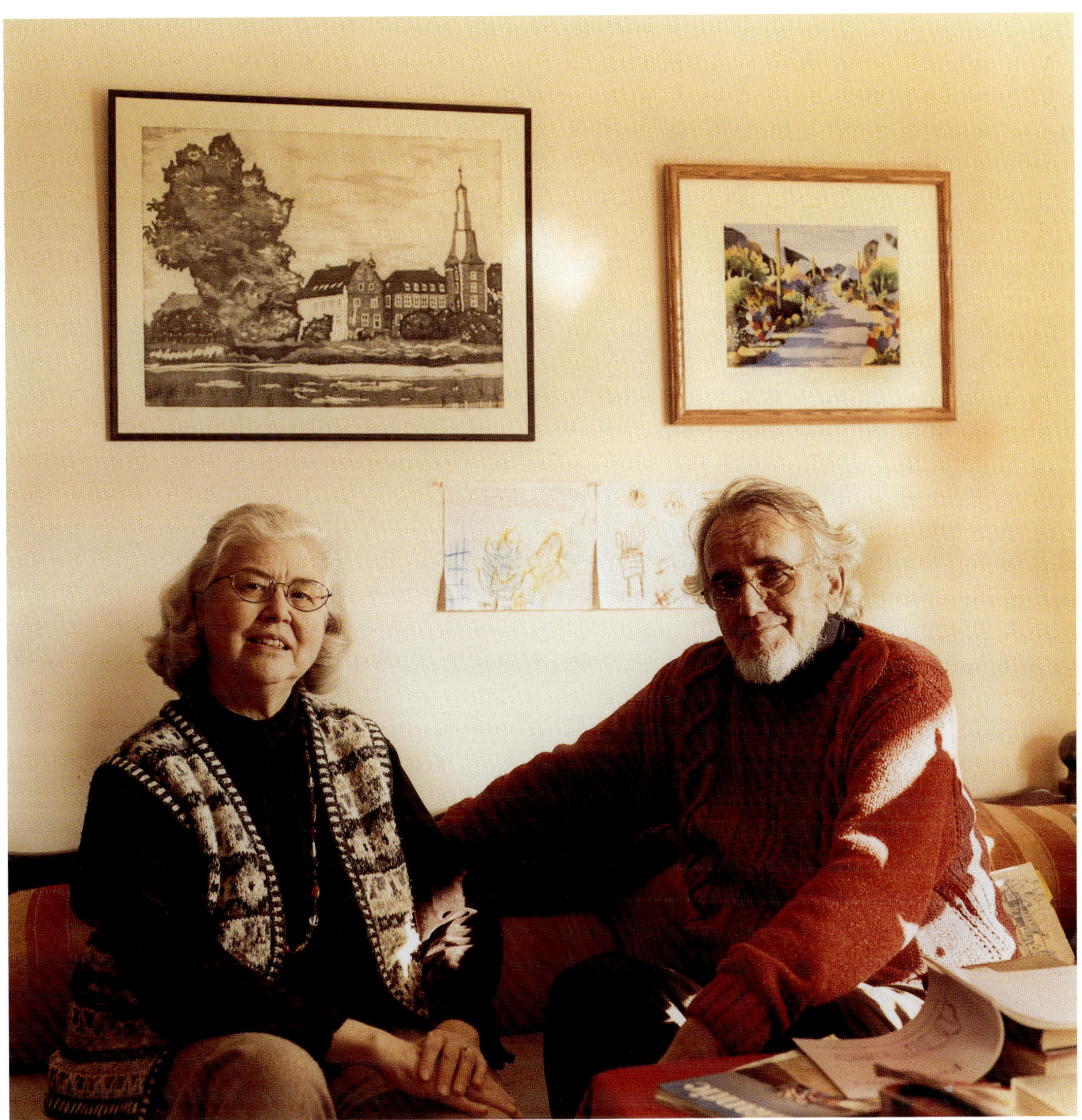

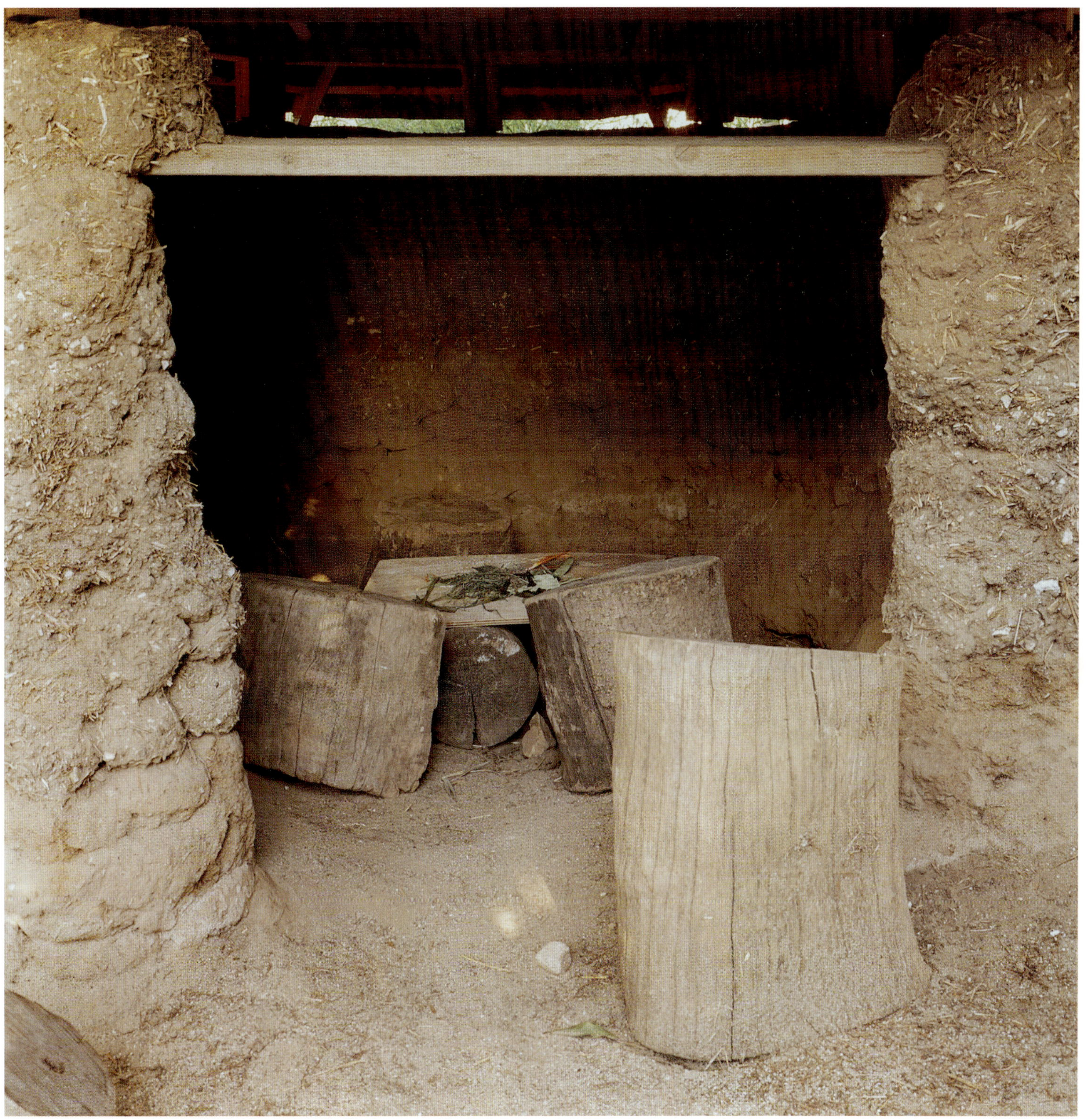

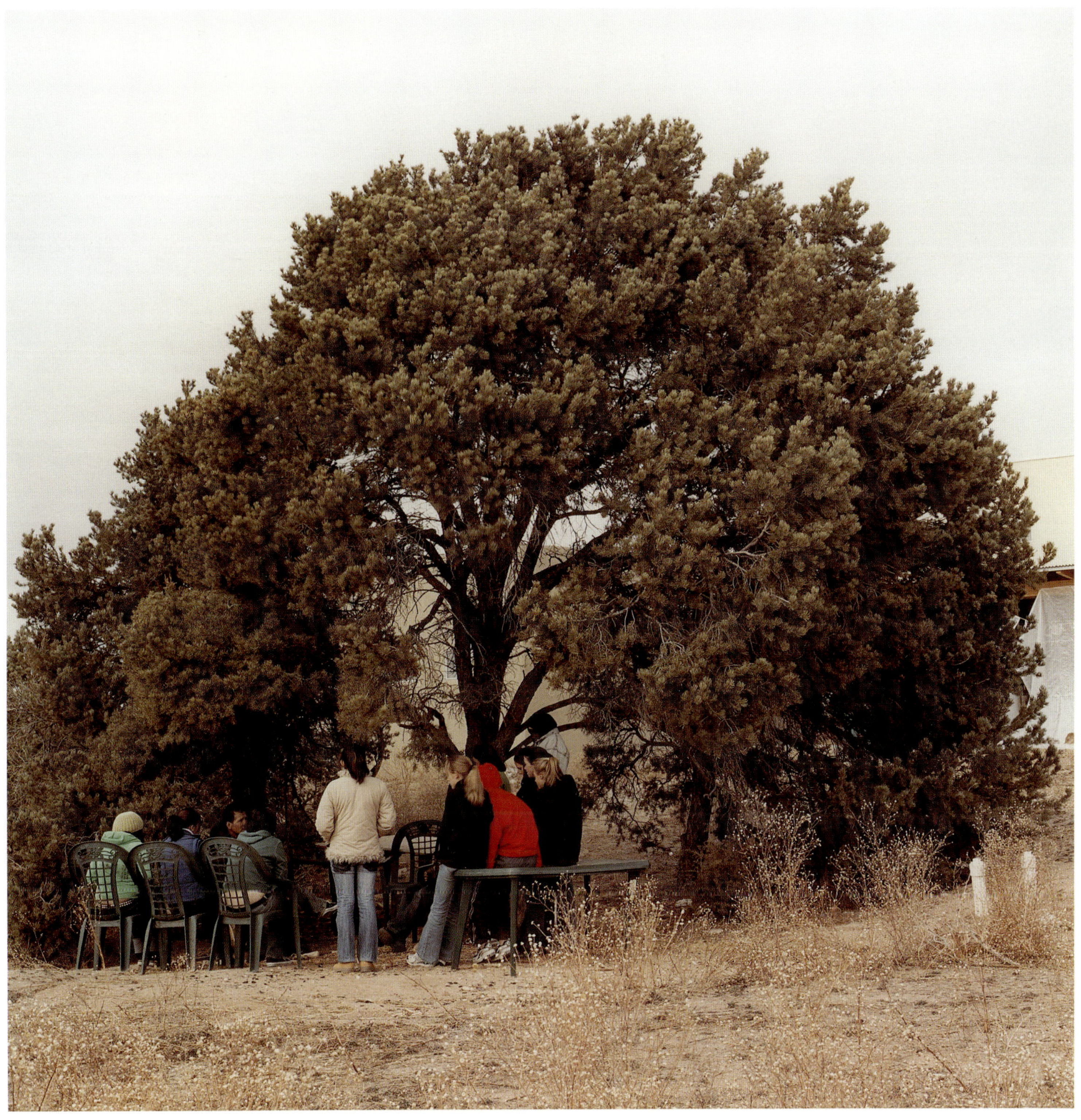

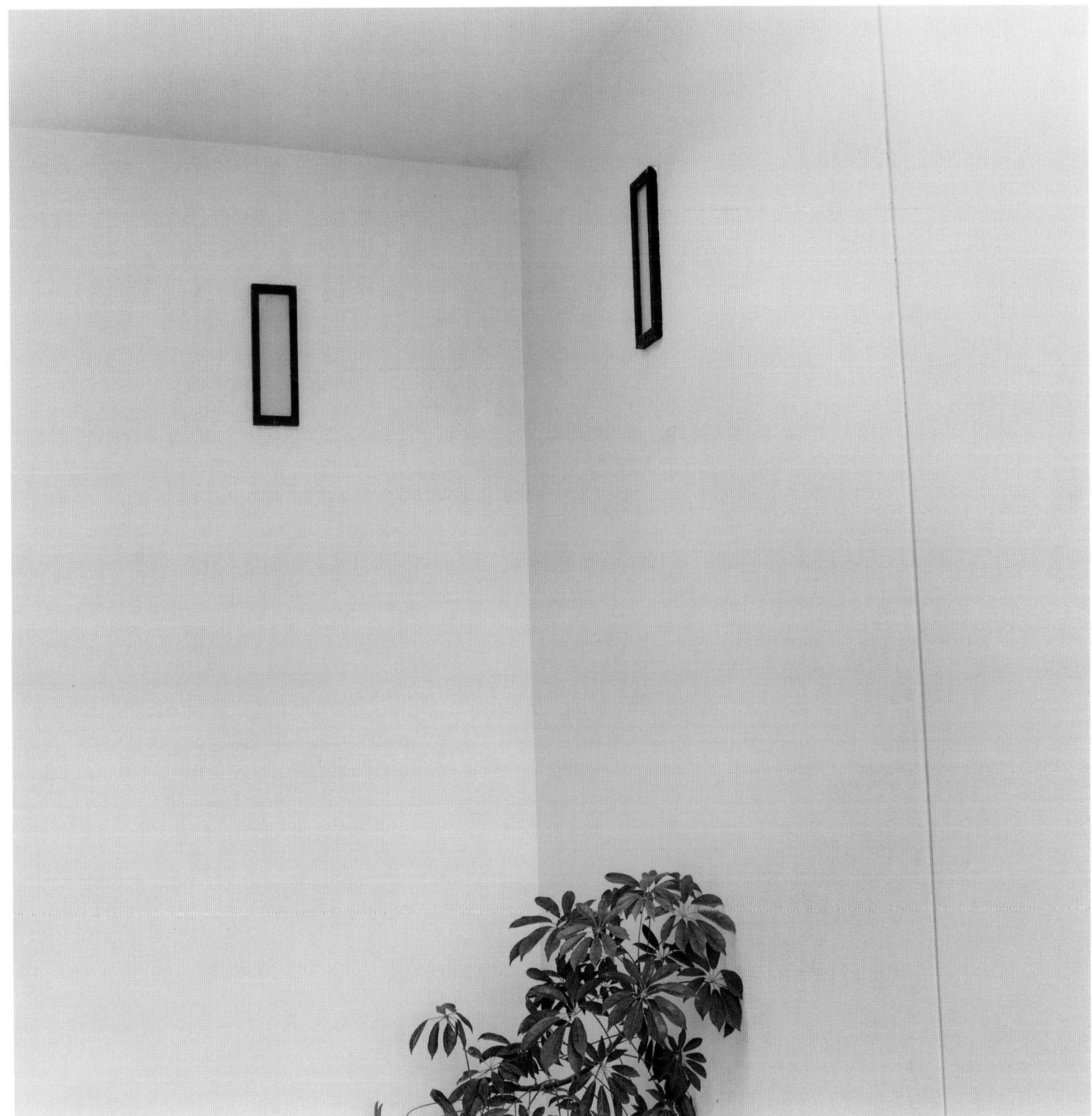

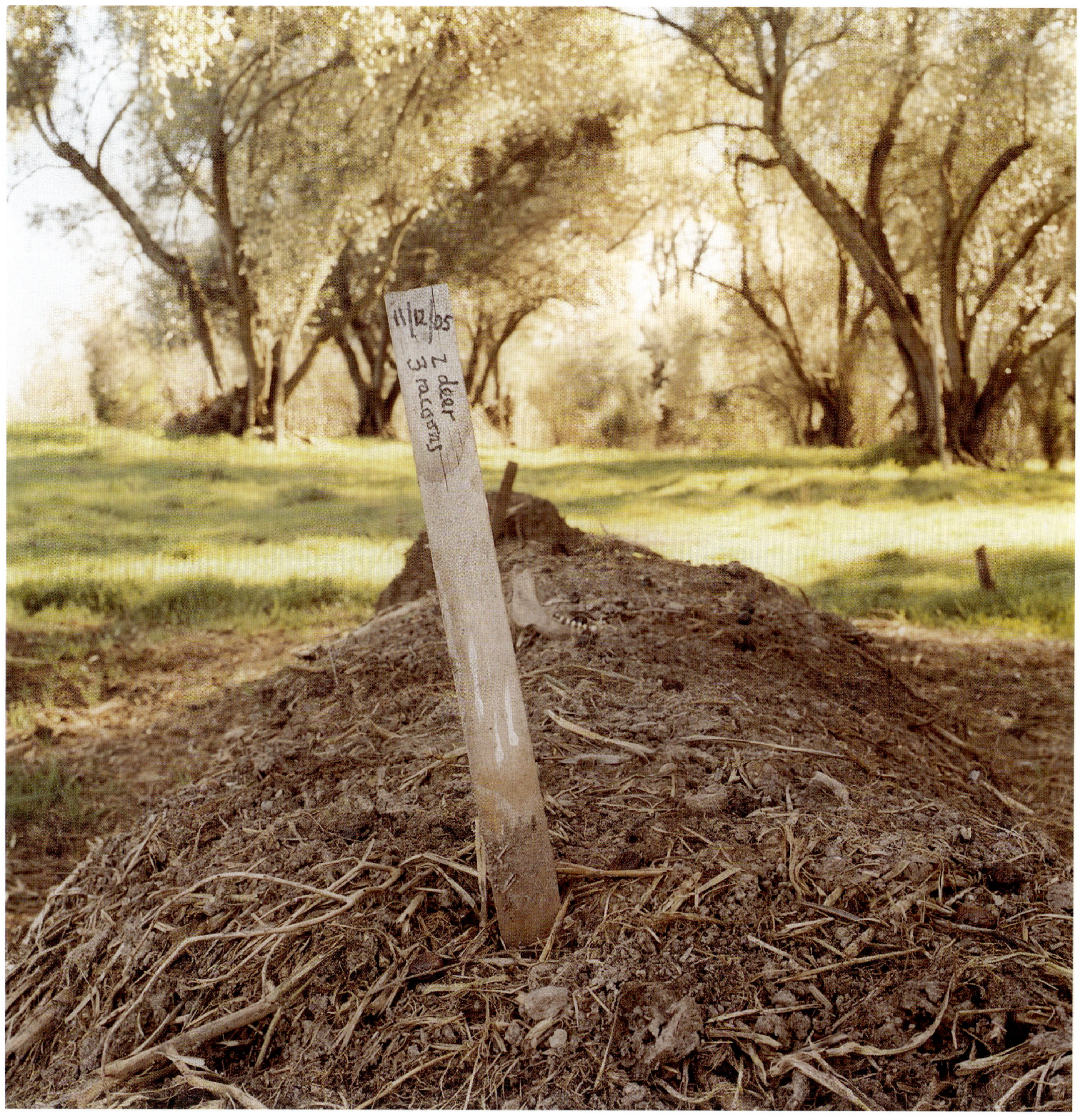

11/12/05
2 deer
3 raccoons

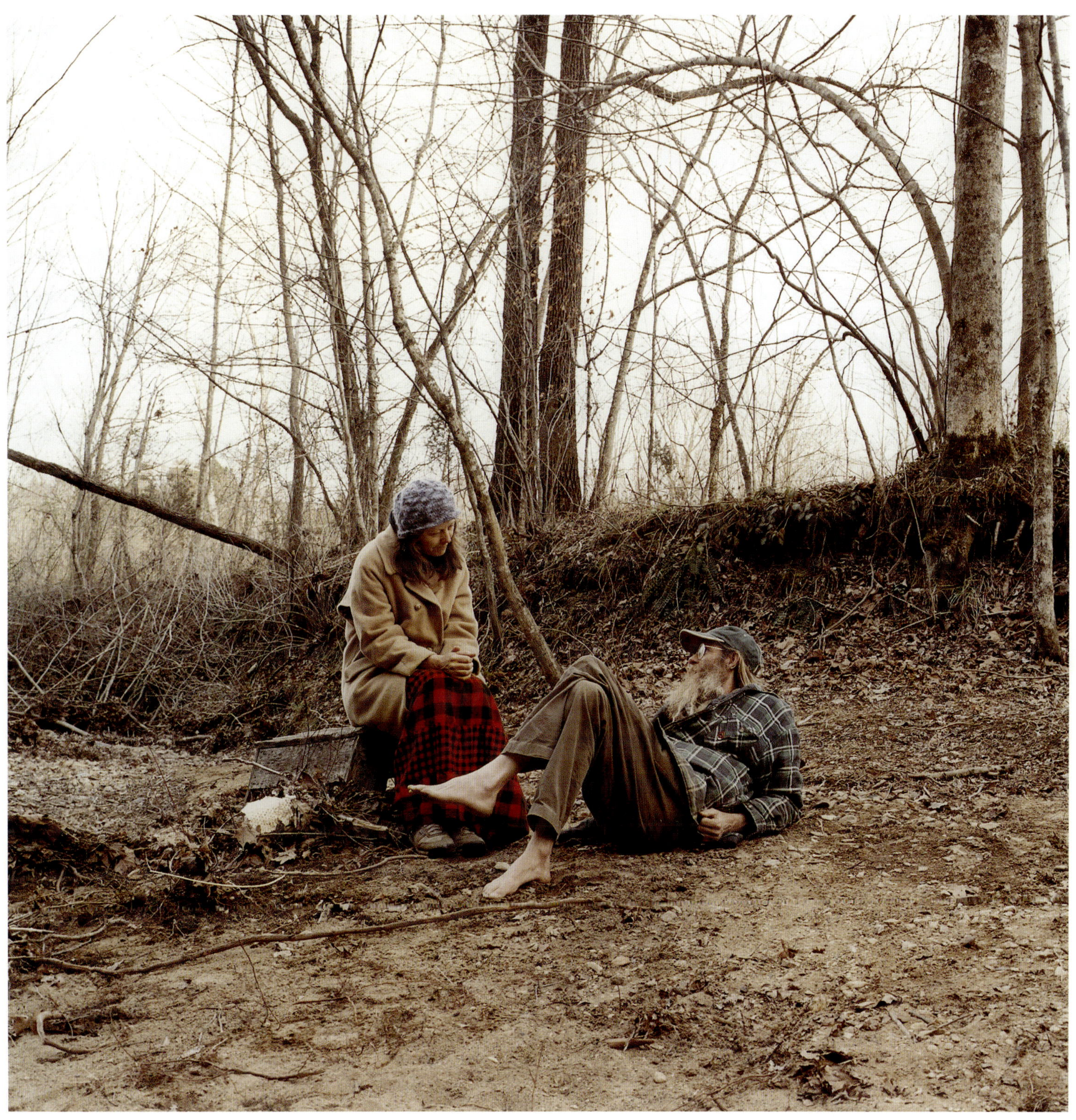

Taj Forer

Taj Forer (b. 1981) lives in Hillsborough, North Carolina, where he serves as a founding editor of _Daylight Magazine_. His photographs have appeared in solo and group exhibitions and are in both private and public collections throughout the United States. Forer has received fellowships from the Rudolf Steiner, Hohenberg, and Mary Duke Biddle Trent Semans Foundations. His work with _Daylight Magazine_ has been awarded multiple grants from LEF Foundation and he was nominated for a United States Artist Fellowship in 2006. Currently, he is an Artist-in-Resident at North Carolina's Contemporary Art Museum.

Solo Exhibitions

2007
  Threefold Sun, Branch Gallery, Durham, North Carolina

2005
  Still Asia, Chapel Hill, North Carolina

2003
  _Co-op_, Artspace Gallery, Bronxville, New York

2002
  Traces, Artspace Gallery, Bronxville, New York

Group Exhibitions

2007
  First Snow, John & June Allcott Gallery, Chapel Hill, North Carolina

2006
  Aqua Art Fair, Aqua Hotel, Miami Beach, Florida
  Pleased to Meet You, Branch Gallery, Durham, North Carolina

2005
  Two for the Seesaw, Branch Gallery, Carrboro, North Carolina
  Art Cologne, "New Contemporaries," Cologne, Germany
  3 Day House Show, Harman Gallery, Chapel Hill, North Carolina

2004
  Landscape, Bolin Creek Cooperative, Carrboro, North Carolina
  nada Art Fair, Branch Gallery, Miami, Florida

2003
  Documentary, Center for Documentary Studies, Durham, North Carolina
  6 Art, Artspace Gallery, Bronxville, New York

Publications

2007
  Threefold Sun, Edizioni Charta, Milan, Italy
  Orion Magazine, July–August

2006
  Guernica Magazine, Spring Artist Feature

2005
  Metropolis Magazine, December–January

2000
  Shots Magazine, Fall
  Shots Magazine, Spring

Press

2007
  Ellen Sung, "He Finds Beauty in the Basic," _The News & Observer_, February 11
  Douglas Vuncannon, "Brutal Youth . . . Beautiful Nudes: Three Strong Exhibits in Downtown Durham," _The Independent Weekly_, February 7

Carol Mavor

Carol Mavor is Professor of Art History and Visual History at the University of Manchester, UK. She is the author of three books: _Reading Boyishly: Roland Barthes, J. M. Barrie, Jacques Henri Lartigue, Marcel Proust, and D. W. Winnicott_; _Becoming: The Photographs of Clementina, Viscountess Hawarden_; _Pleasures Taken: Performances of Sexuality and Loss in Victorian Photographs_, all published by Duke University Press. Currently, she is finishing a novel entitled _Full_, and a slim film book entitled _Black and Blue_.

To find out more about Charta, and to learn
about our most recent publications, visit

www.chartaartbooks.it

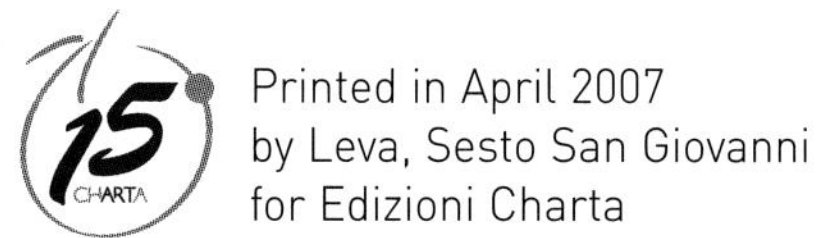

Printed in April 2007
by Leva, Sesto San Giovanni
for Edizioni Charta